Lump Sum Lottery

Bonnie Briant

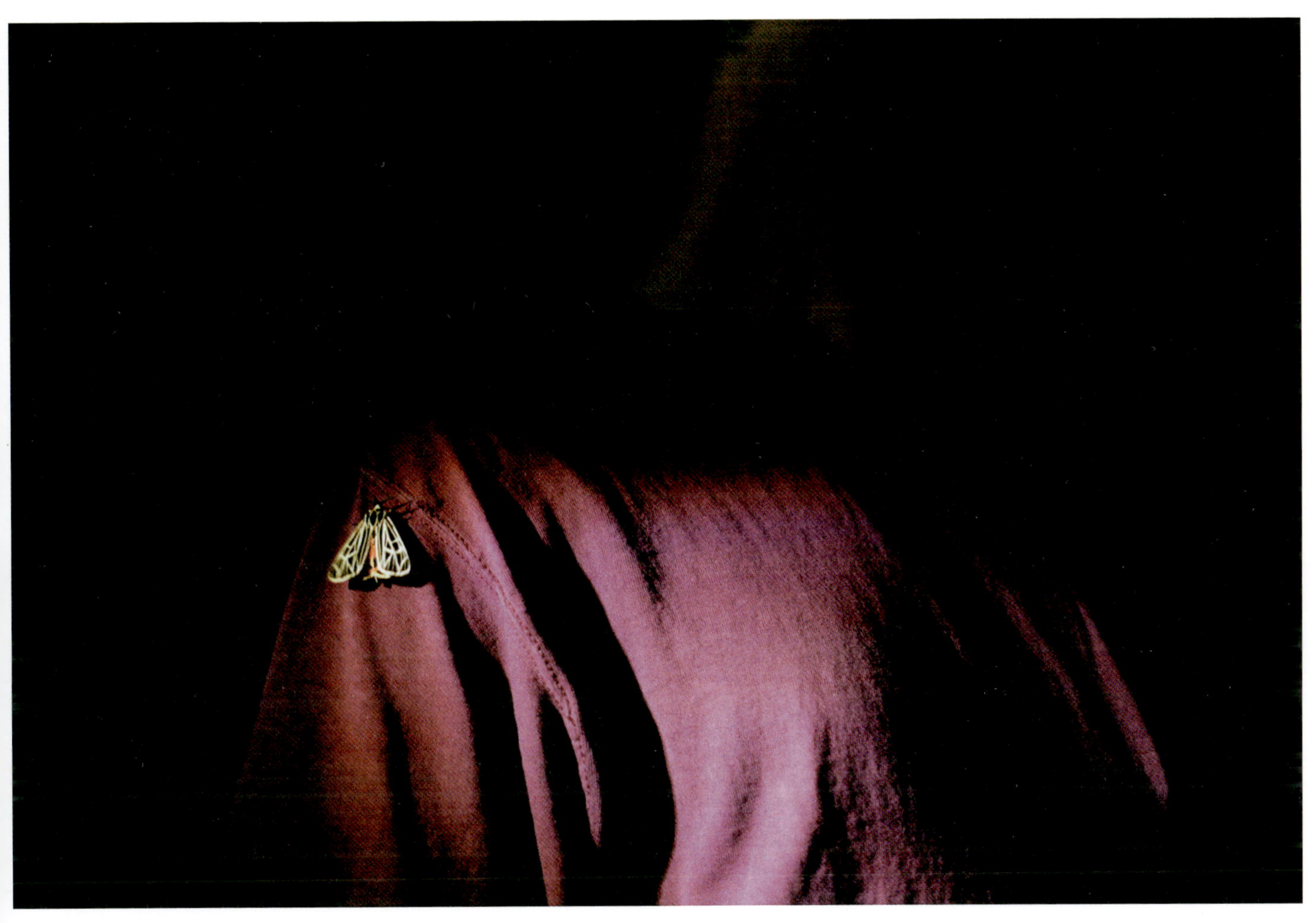

Sylvia Plachy
Wed, Dec 11, 2:47 PM to me

I think
It's charming and disturbing, alienated yet not
lonely. Lost and submerged in colors and
light, rhythms and patterns in a seemingly endless
late afternoon inside a world that is indifferent.

Sylvia Plachy
Wed, Dec 11, 2:52 PM to me

It's 21st century Ennui

Sylvia Plachy
Thu, Dec 12, 10:11 AM to me

Today is the morning after the first impressions
and I woke up in my friend's beautiful house
and took a bunch of pictures fresh from my sleep,
and it came to me: what your book is about
is the "the solace of seeing."

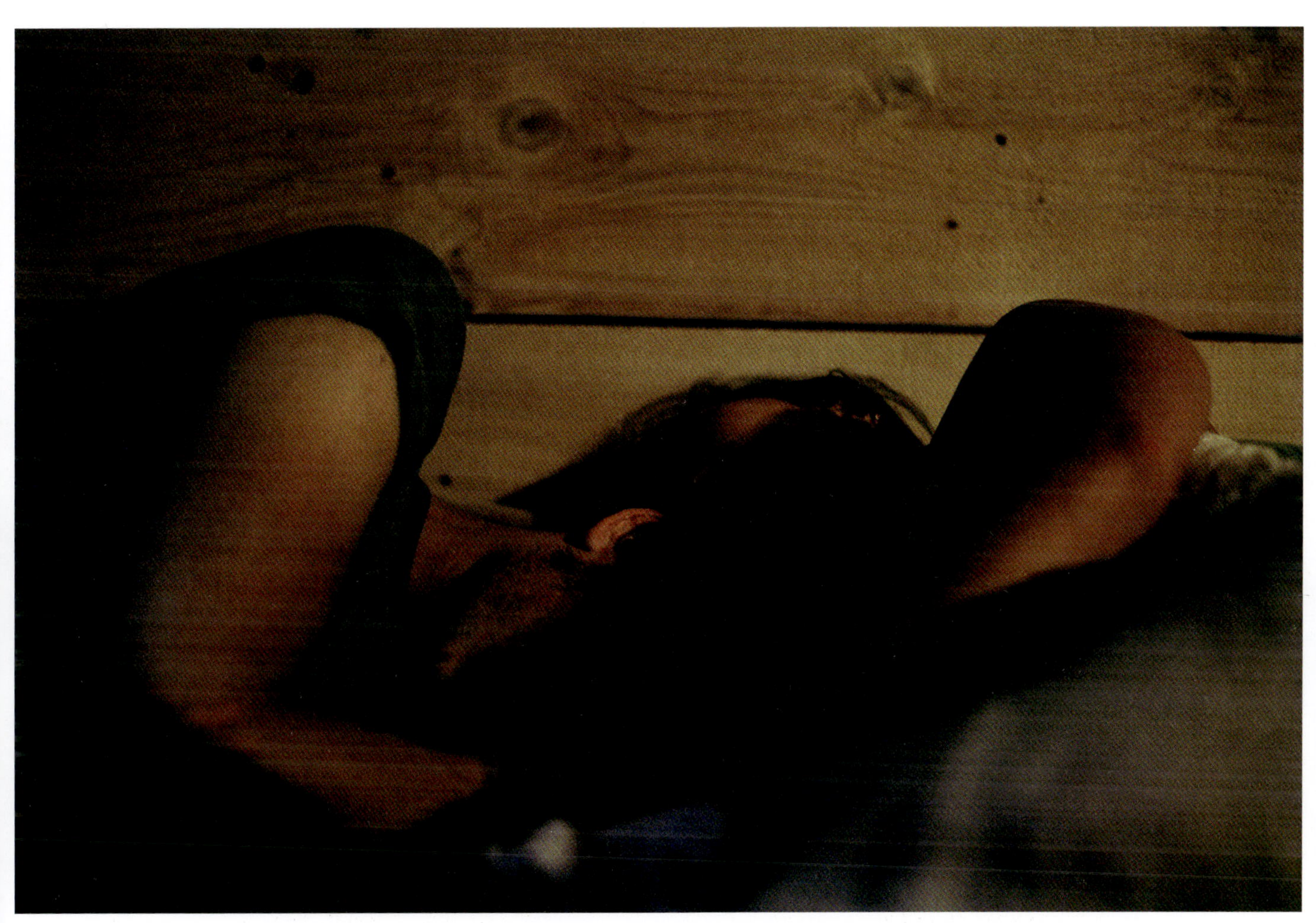

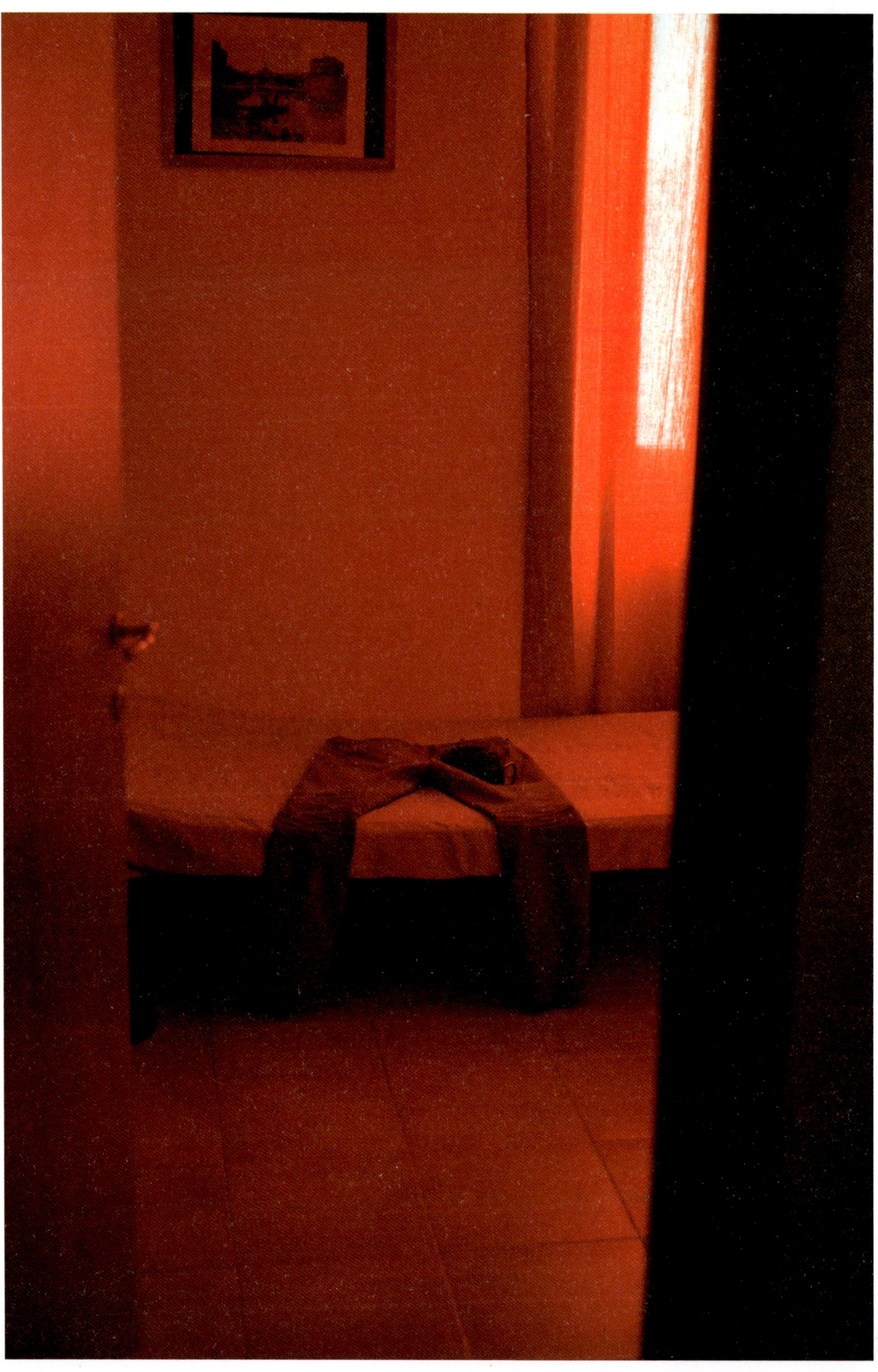

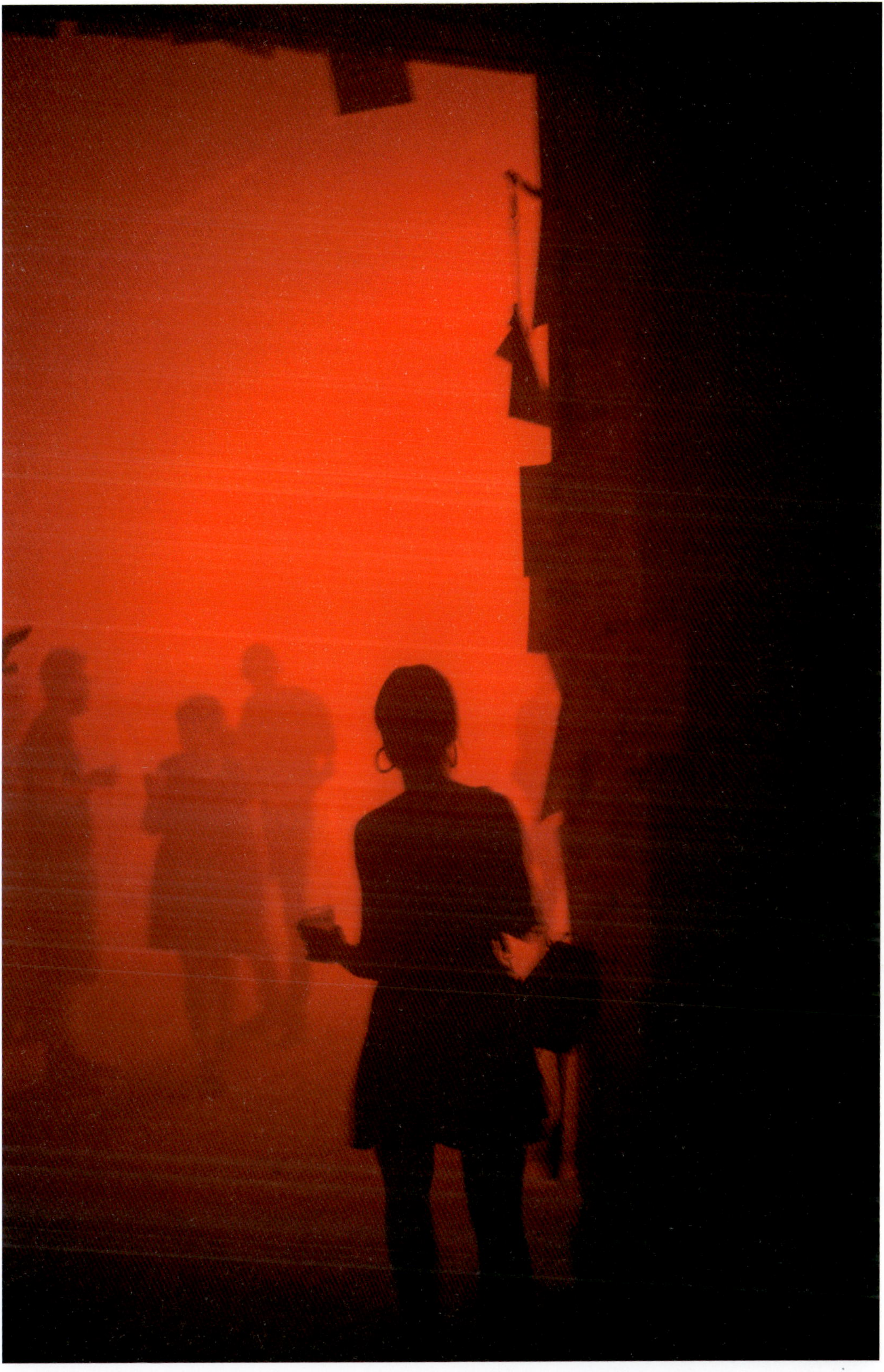

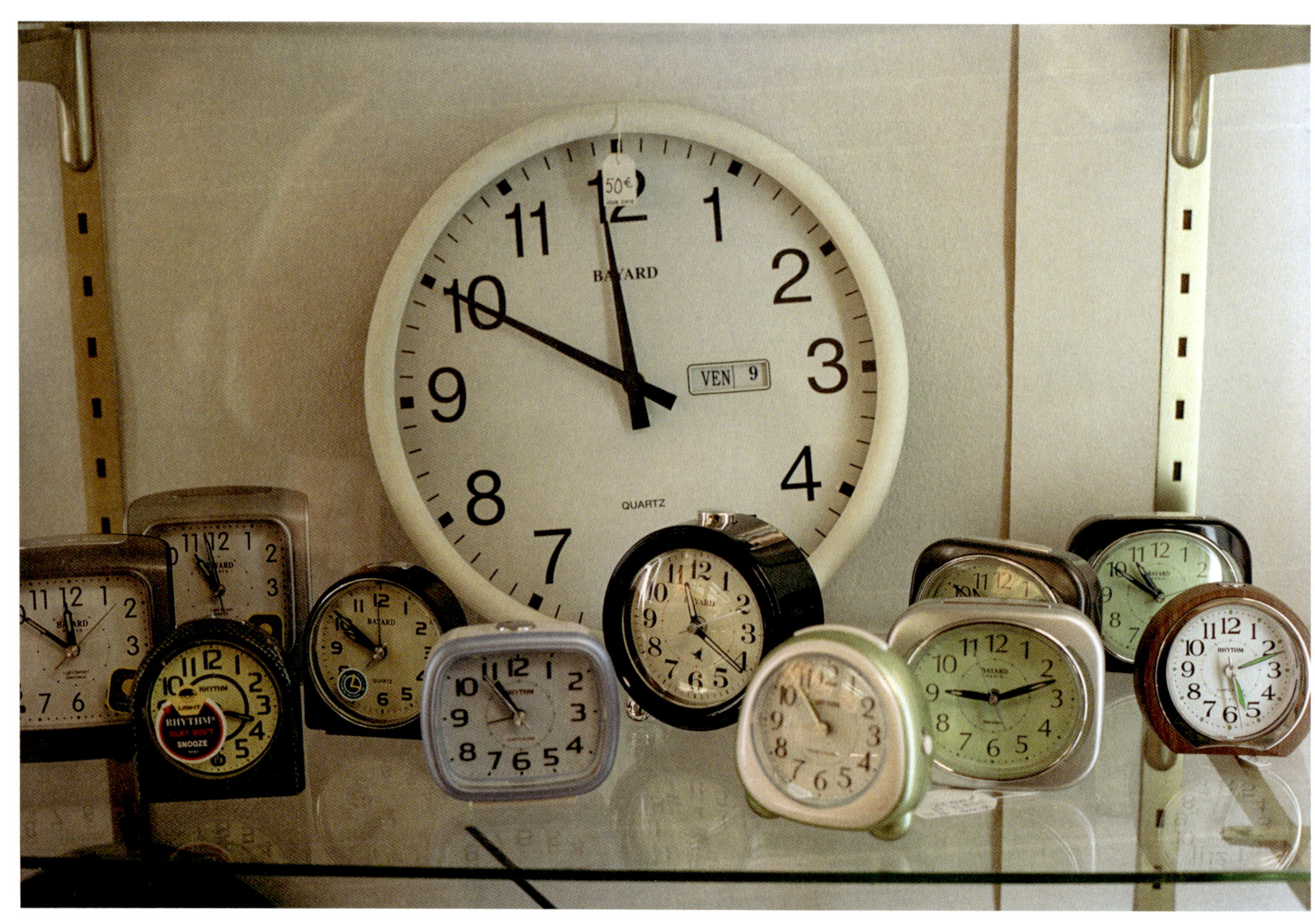

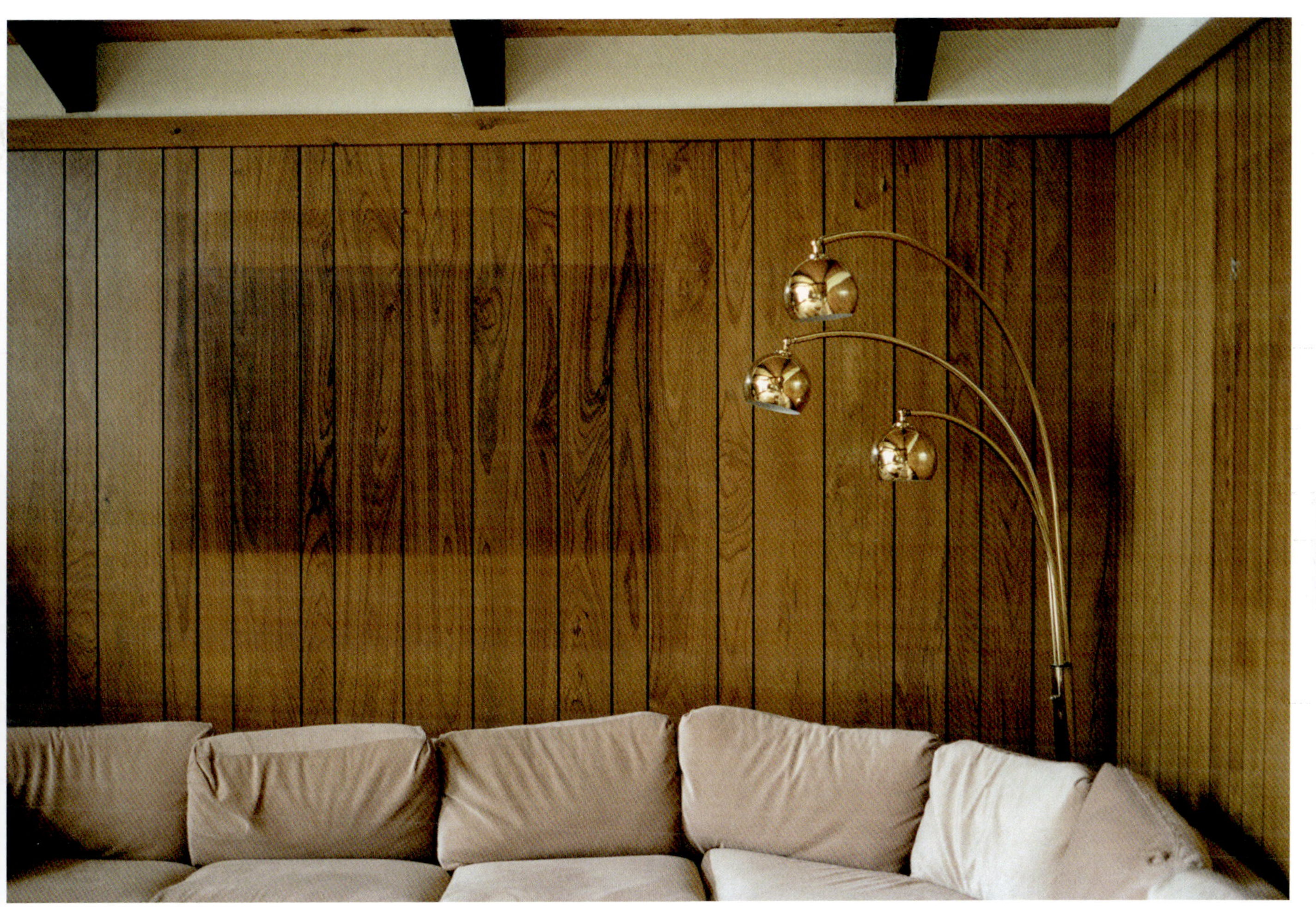

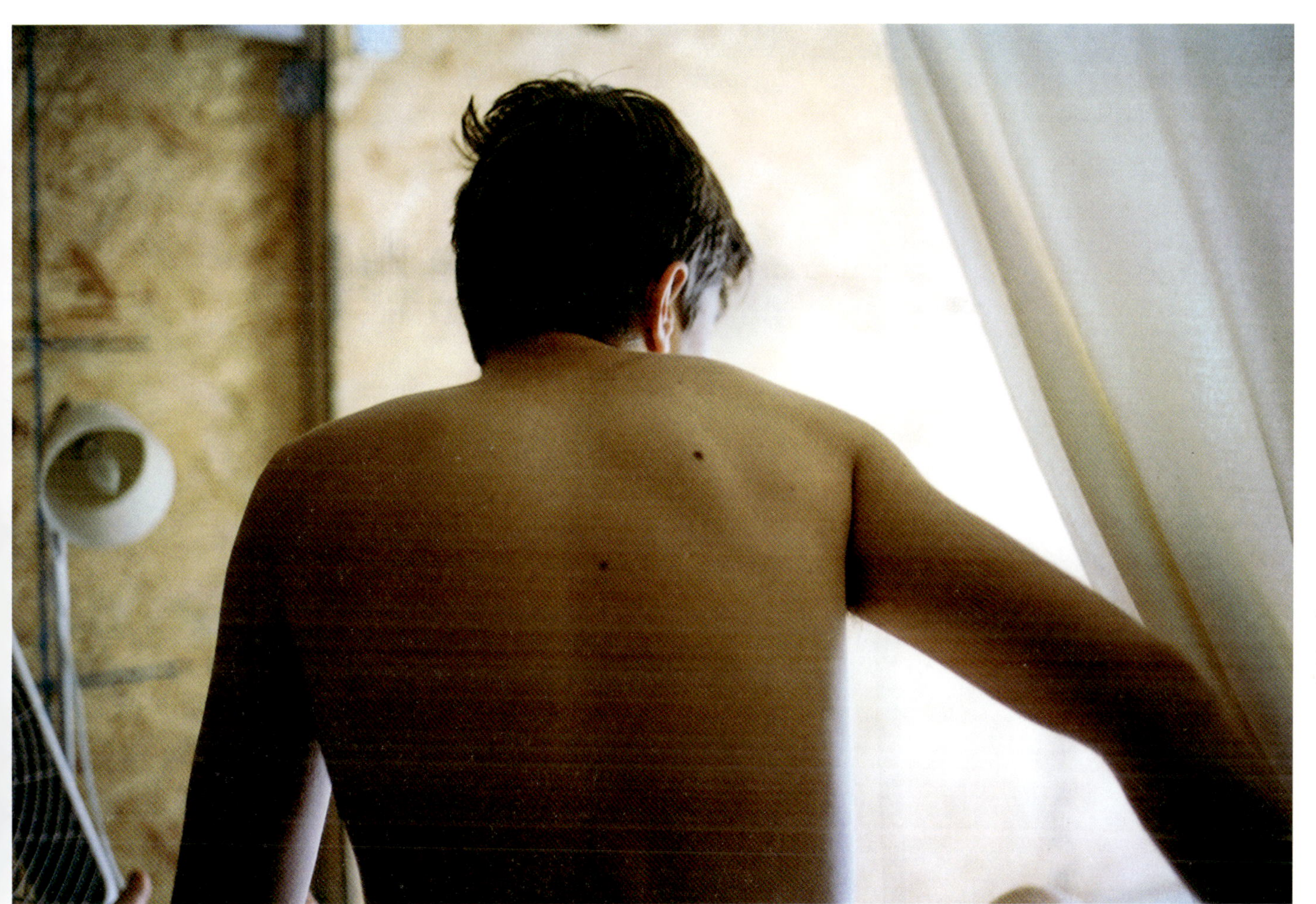

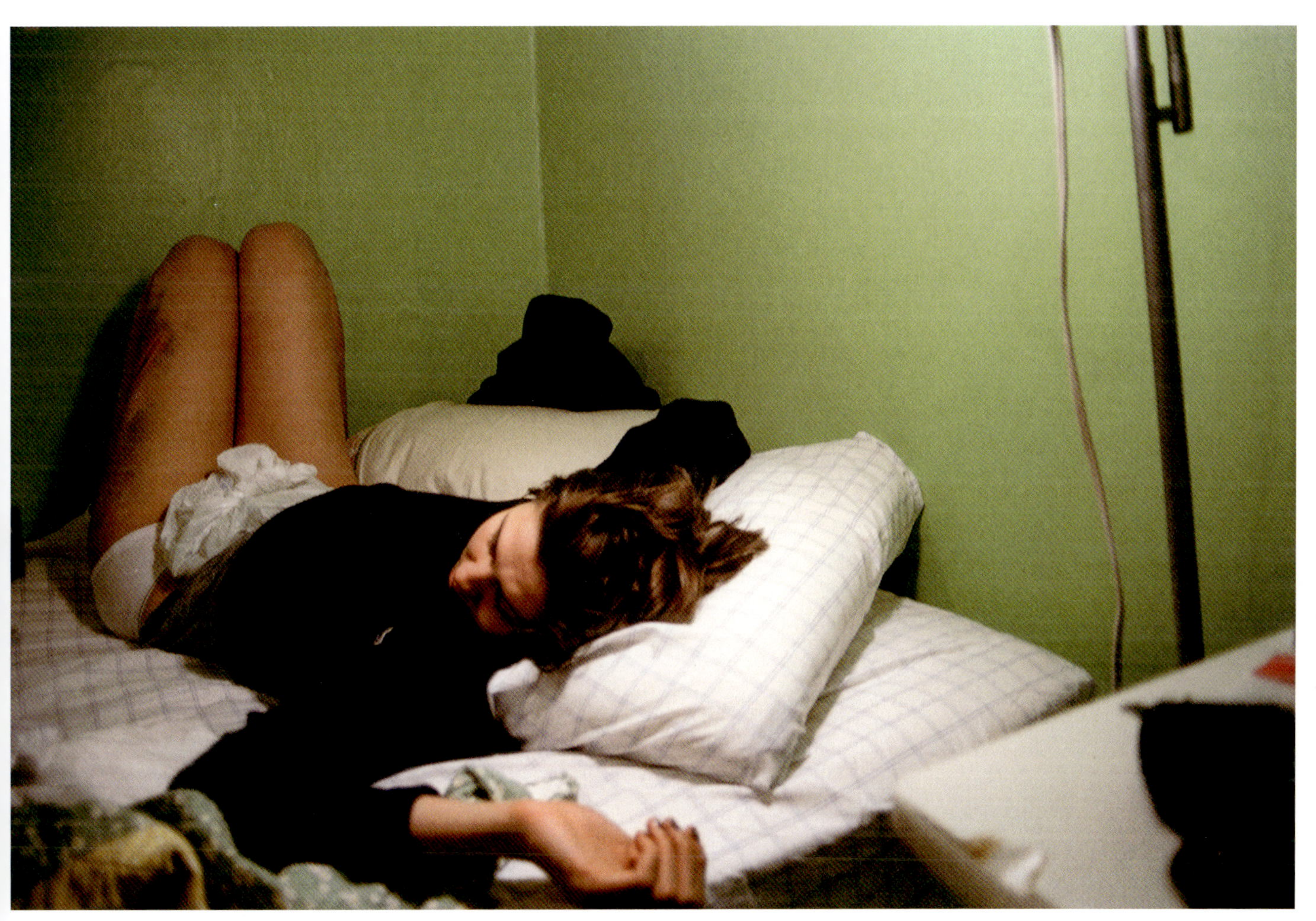

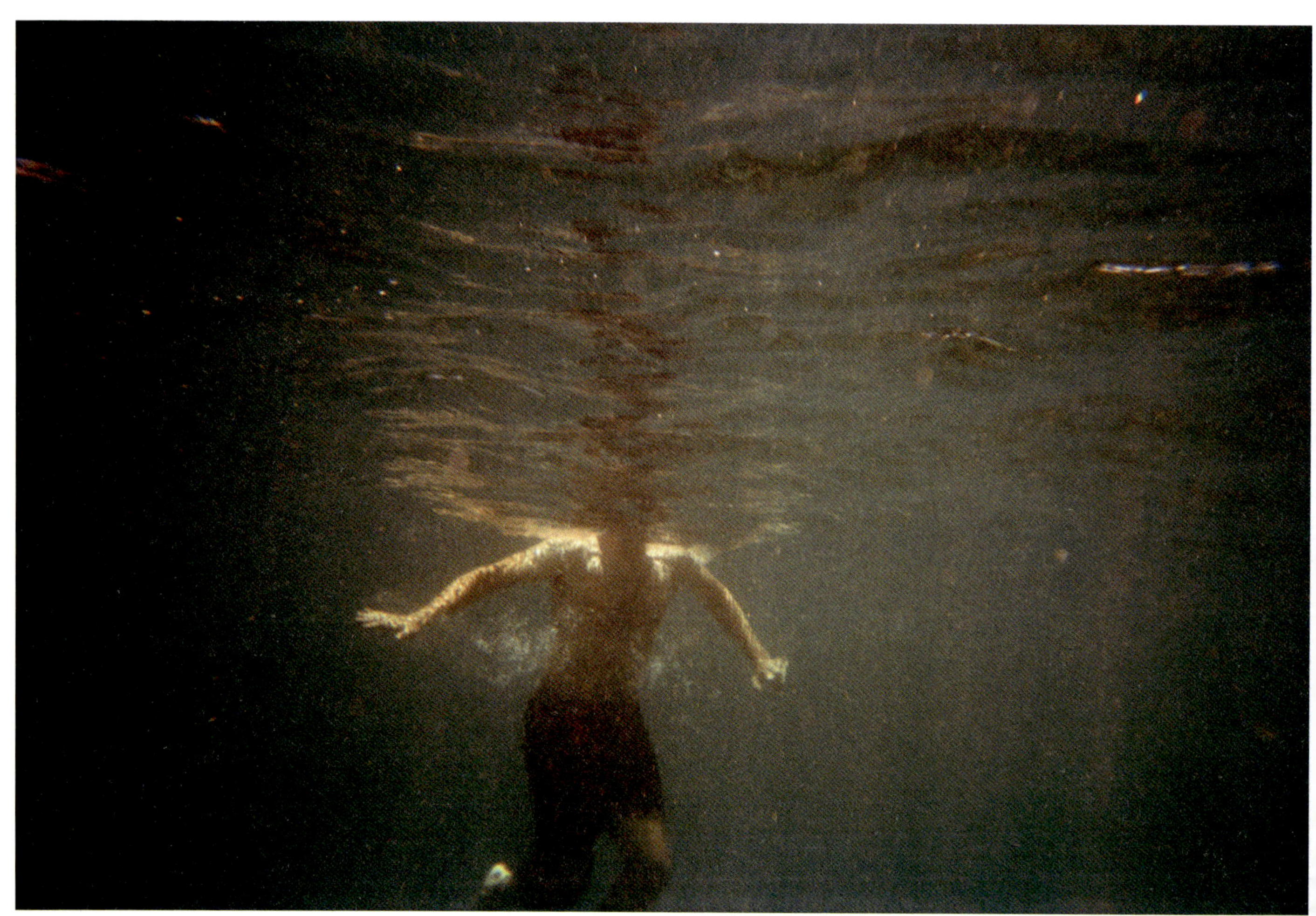

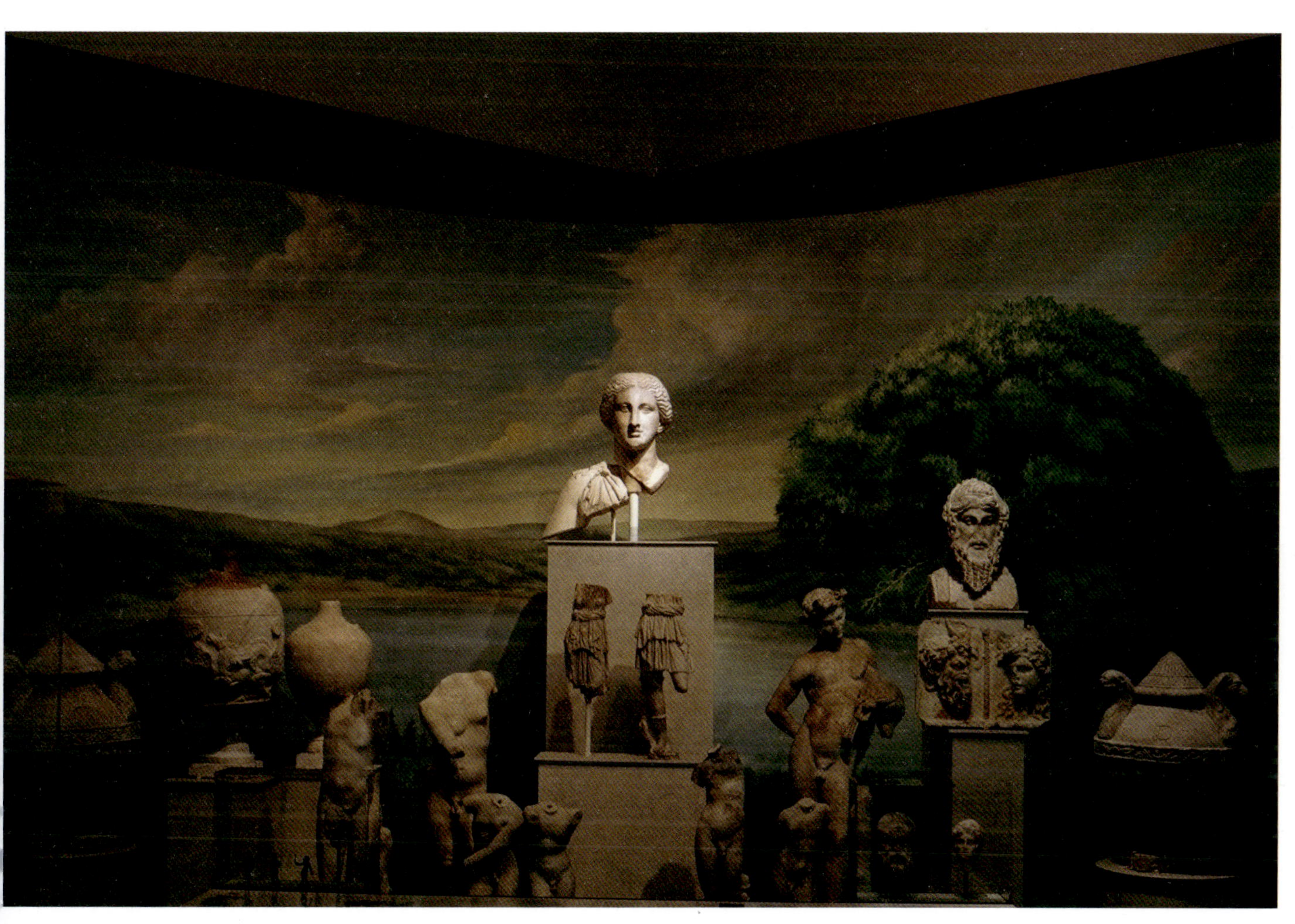

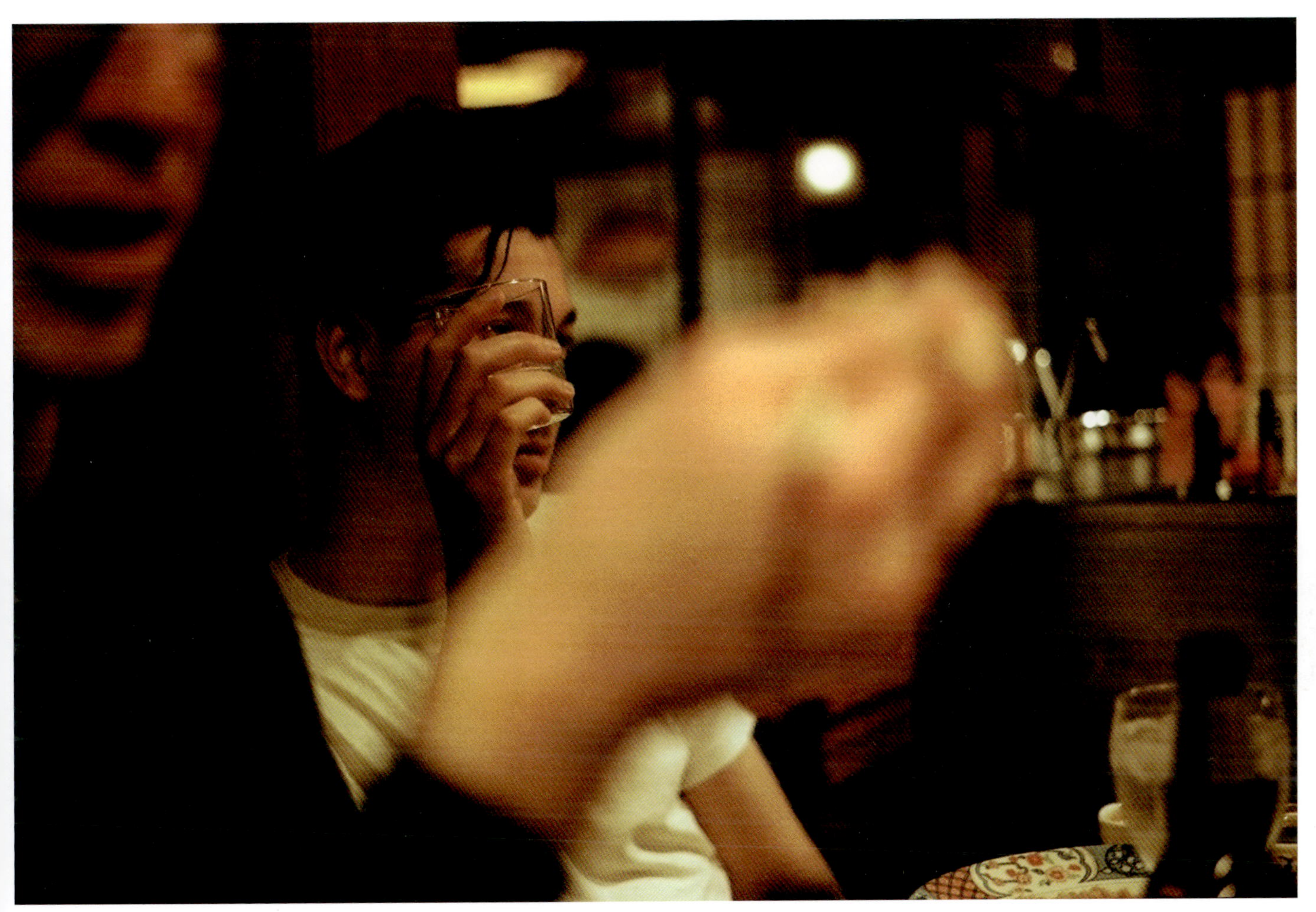

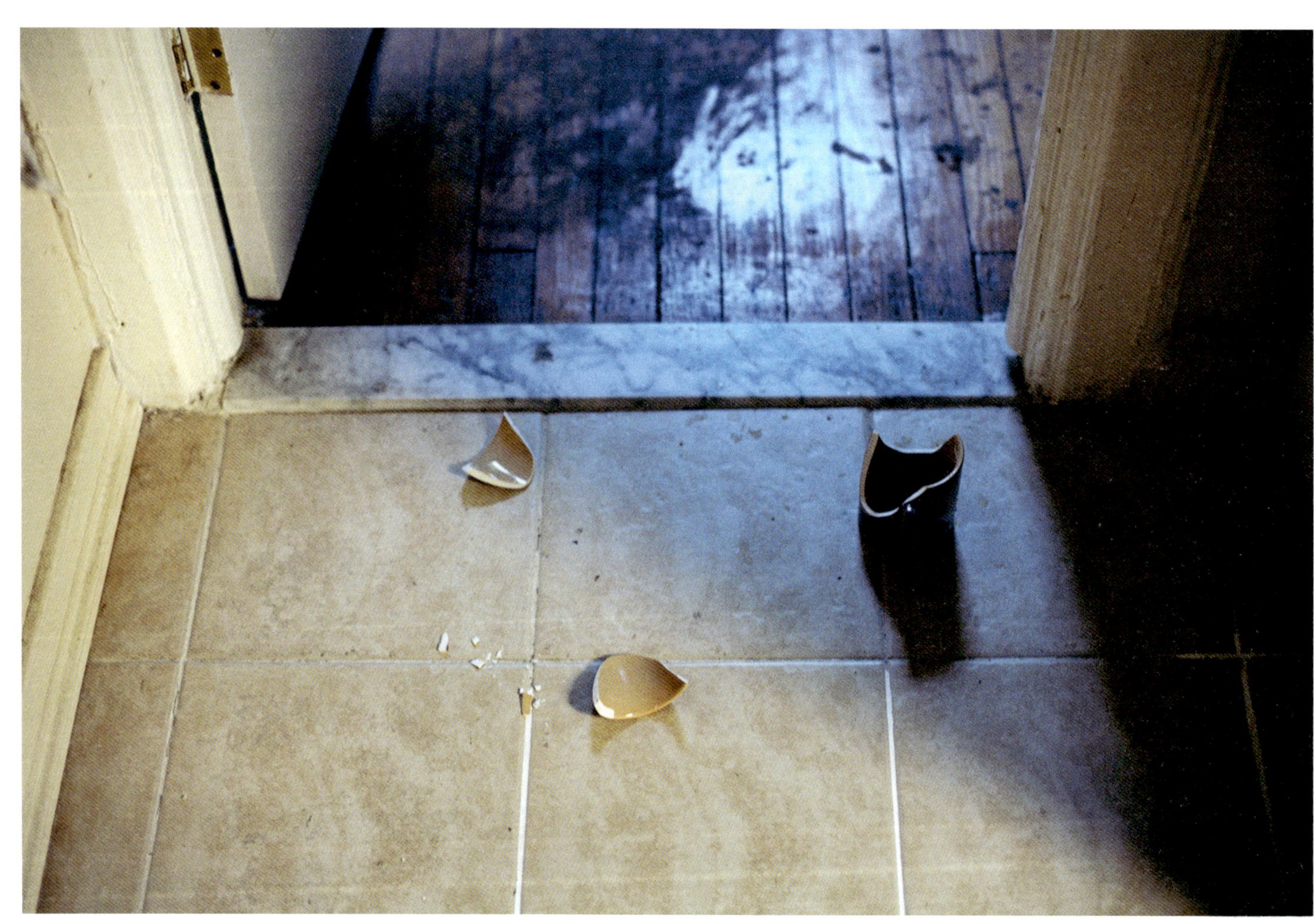

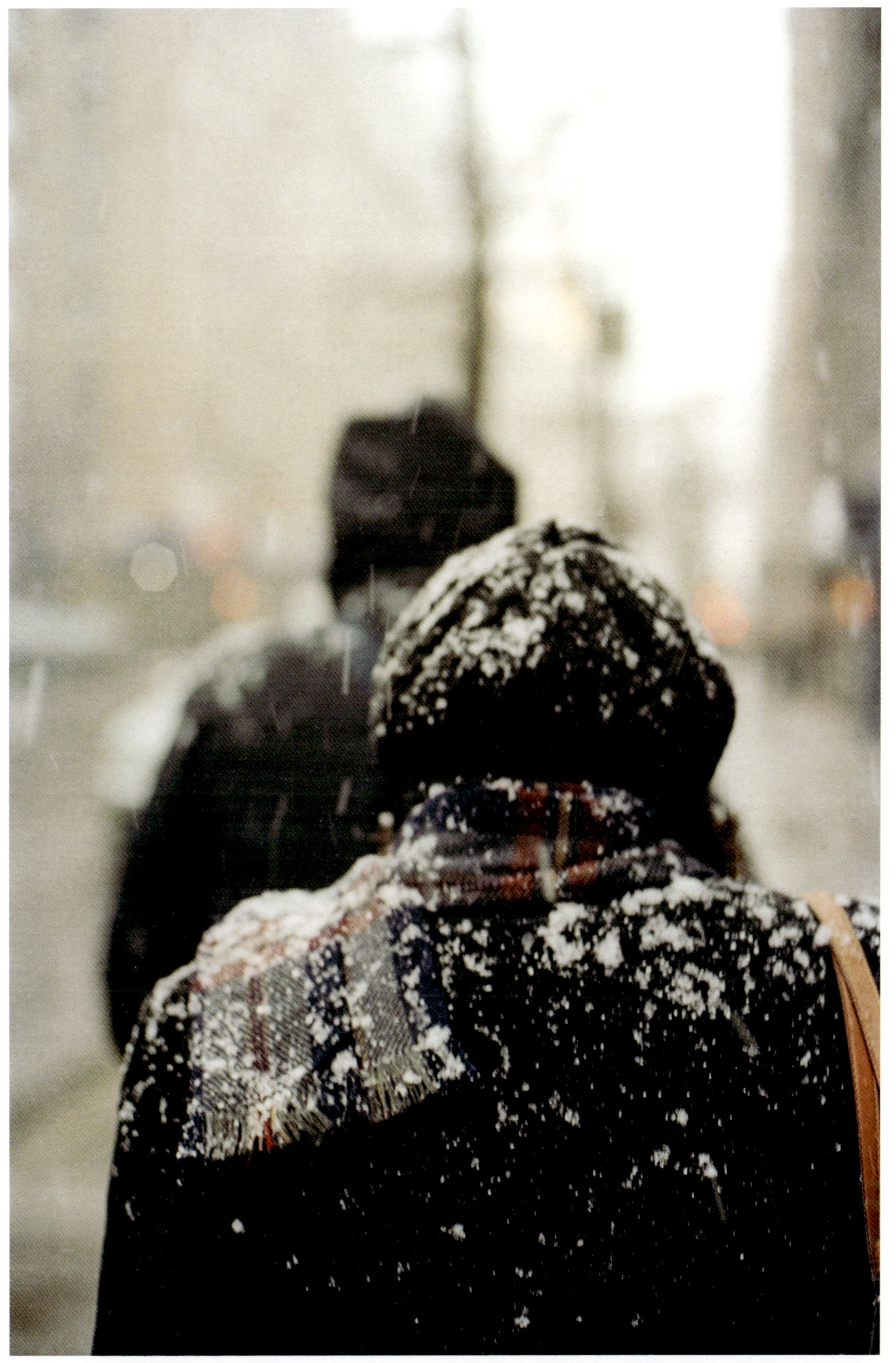

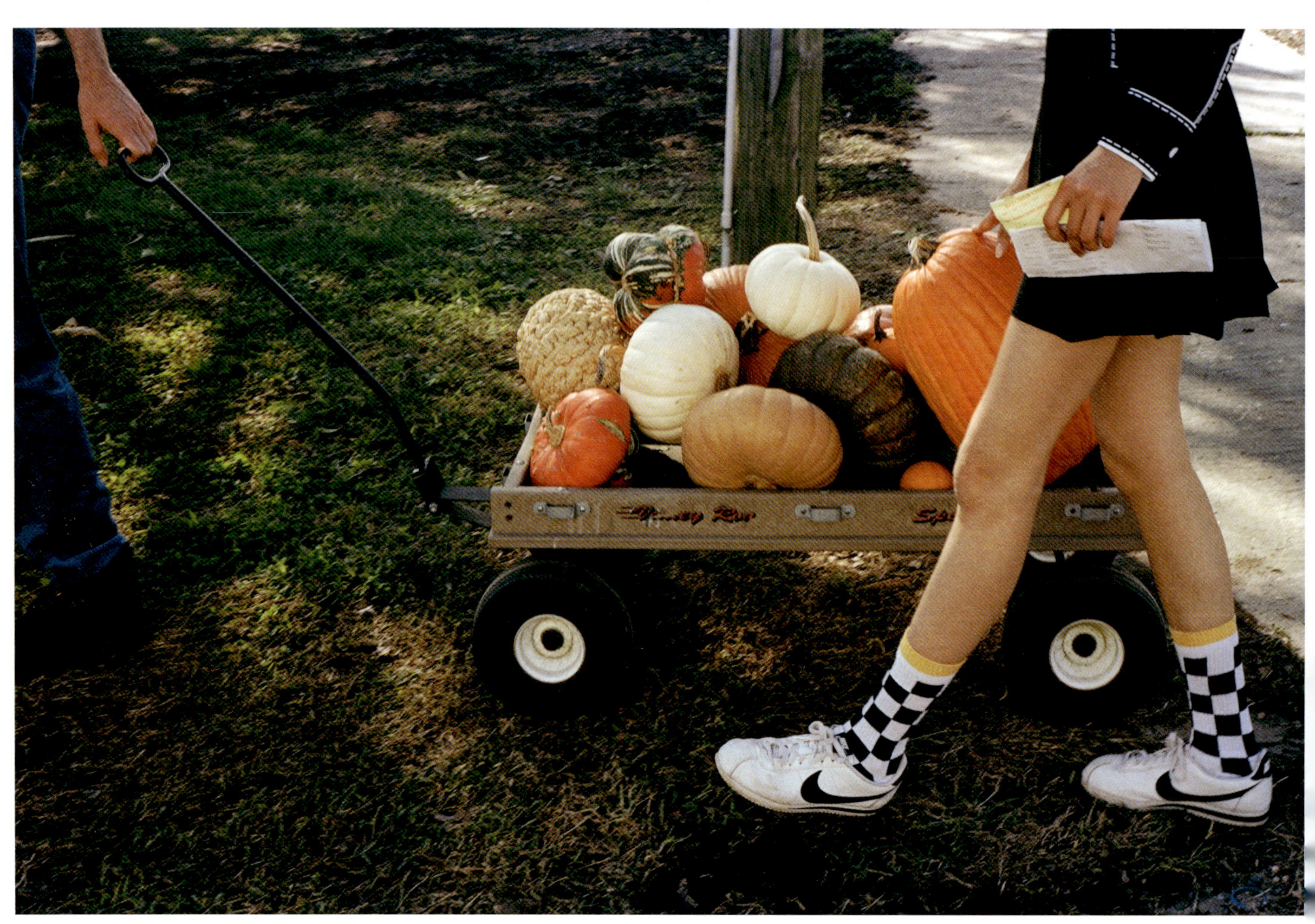

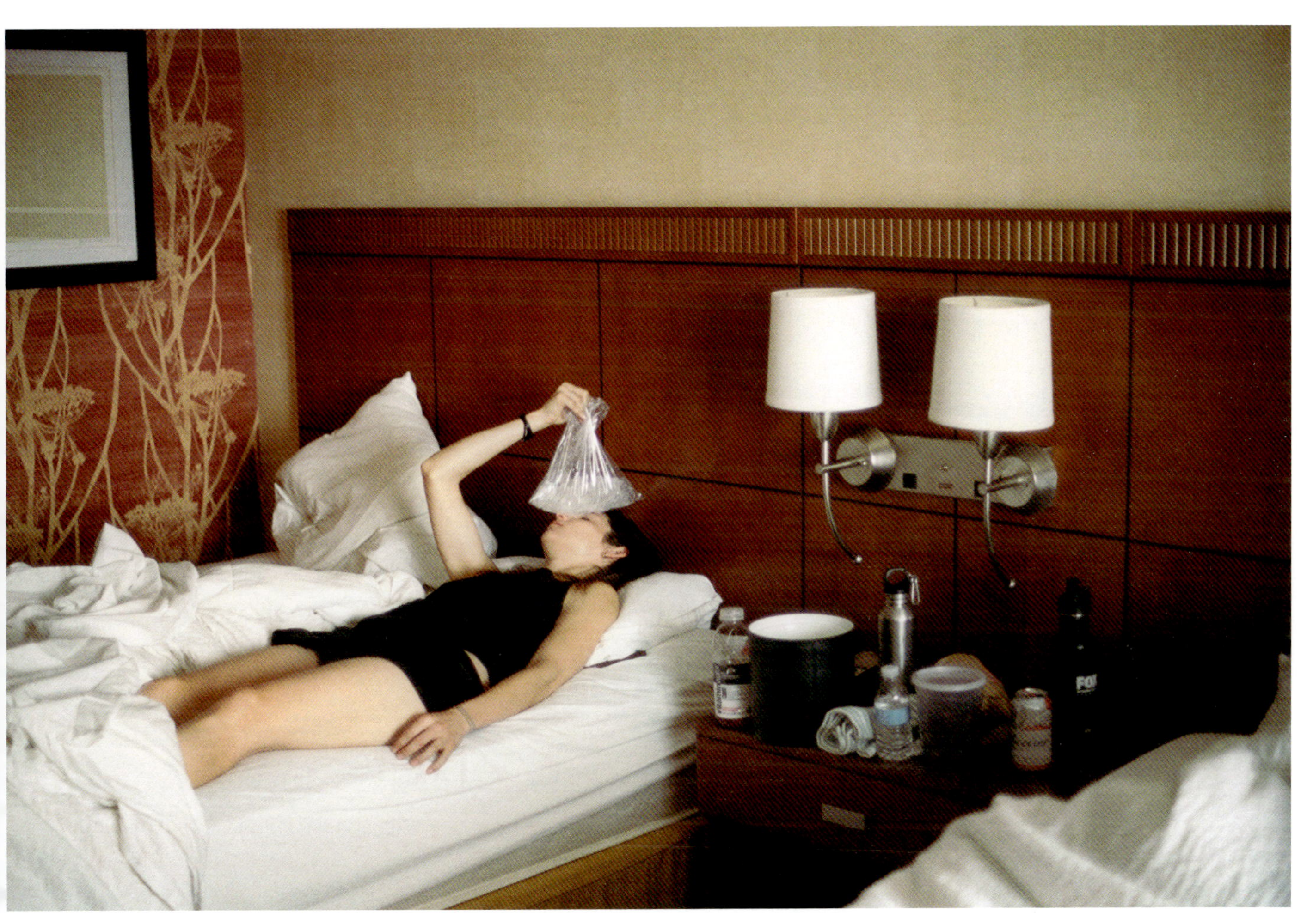

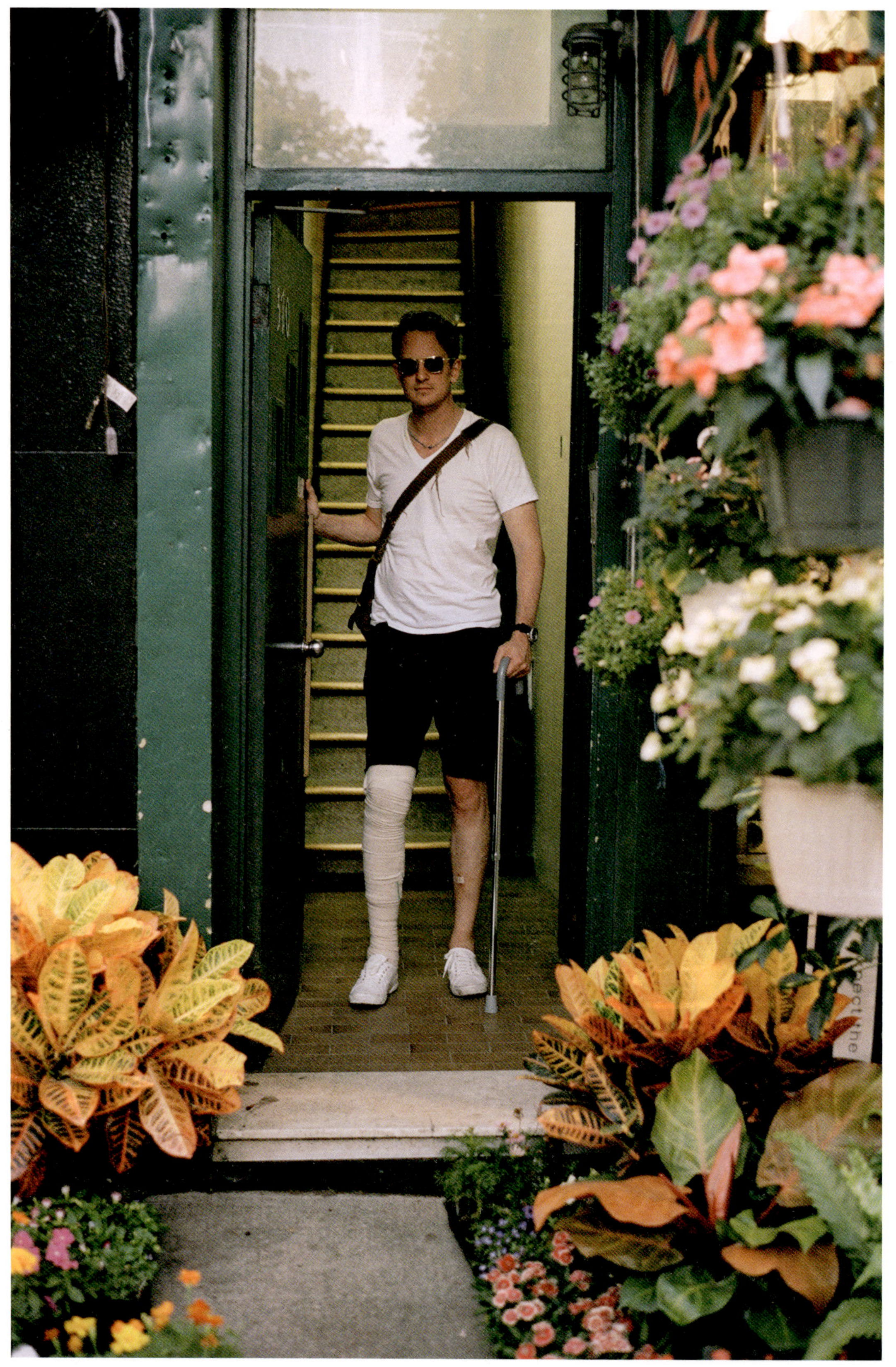

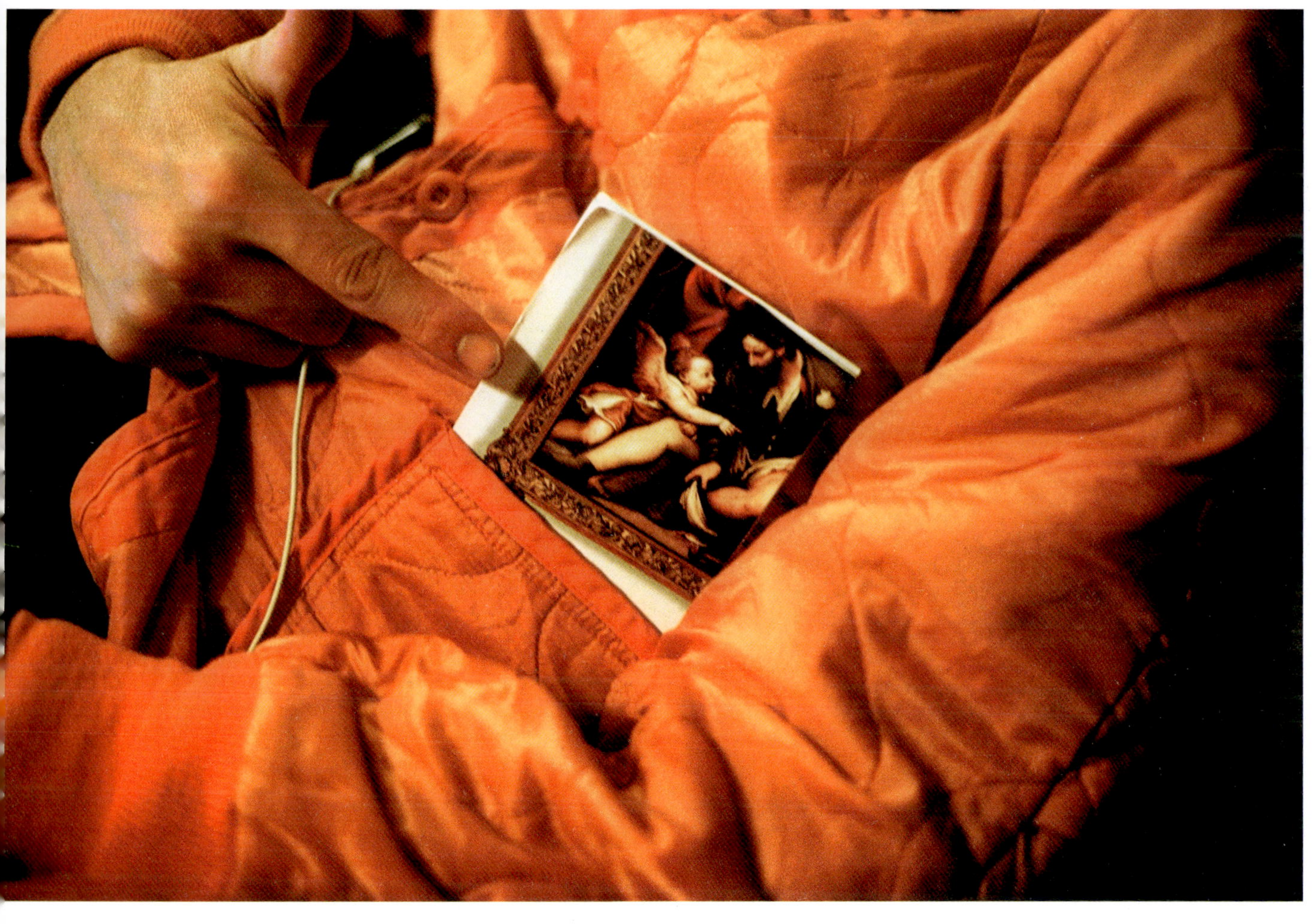

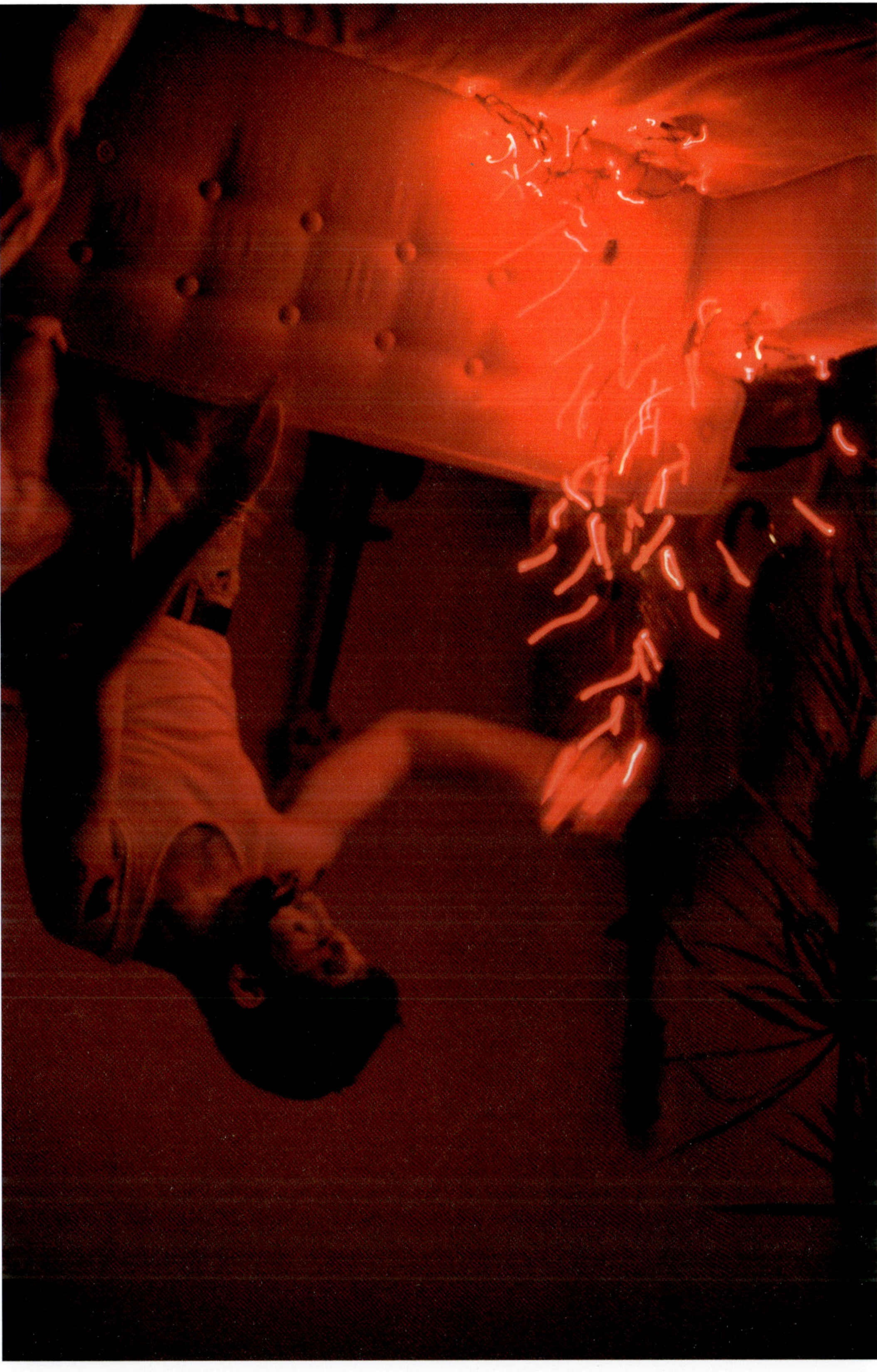

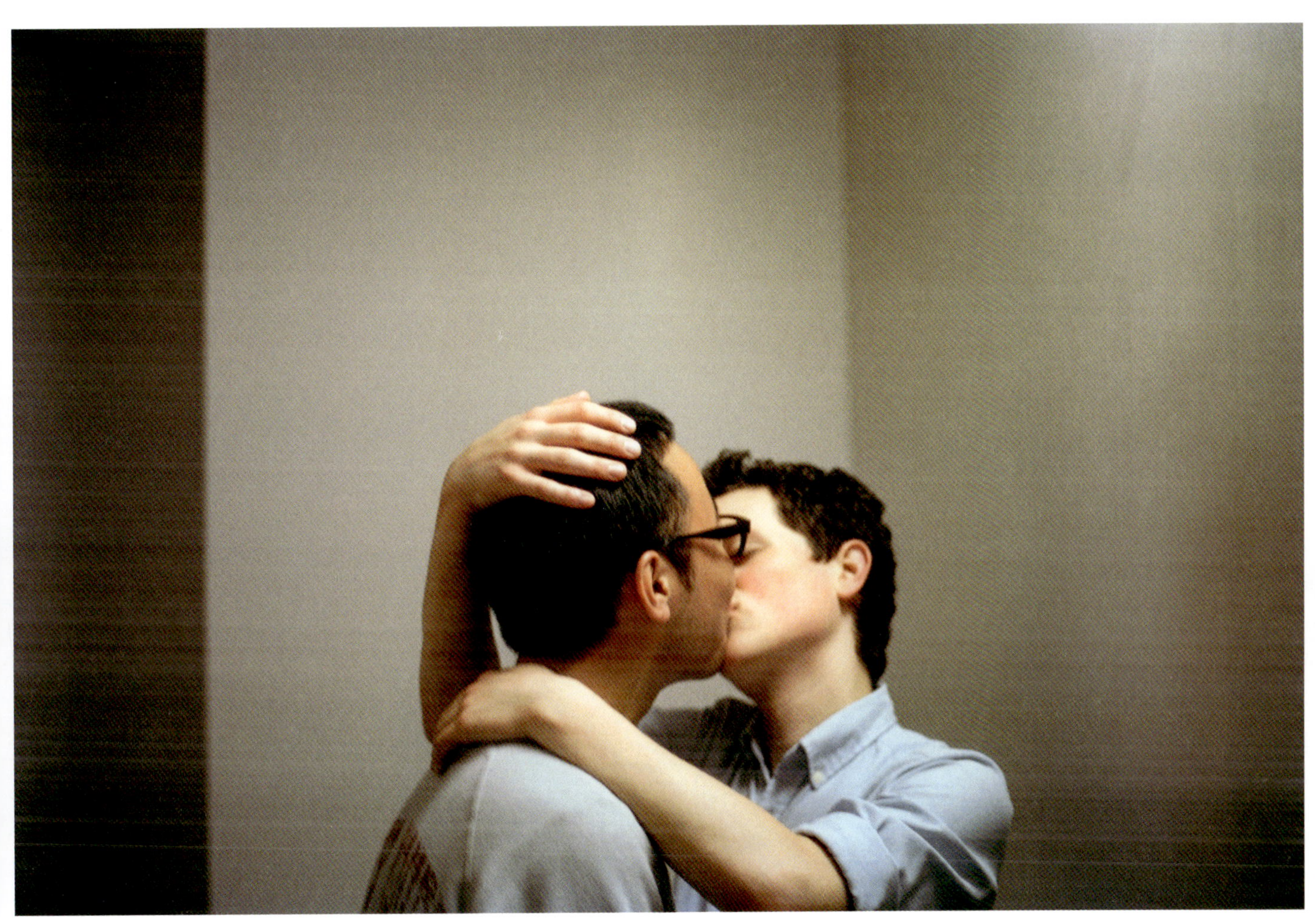

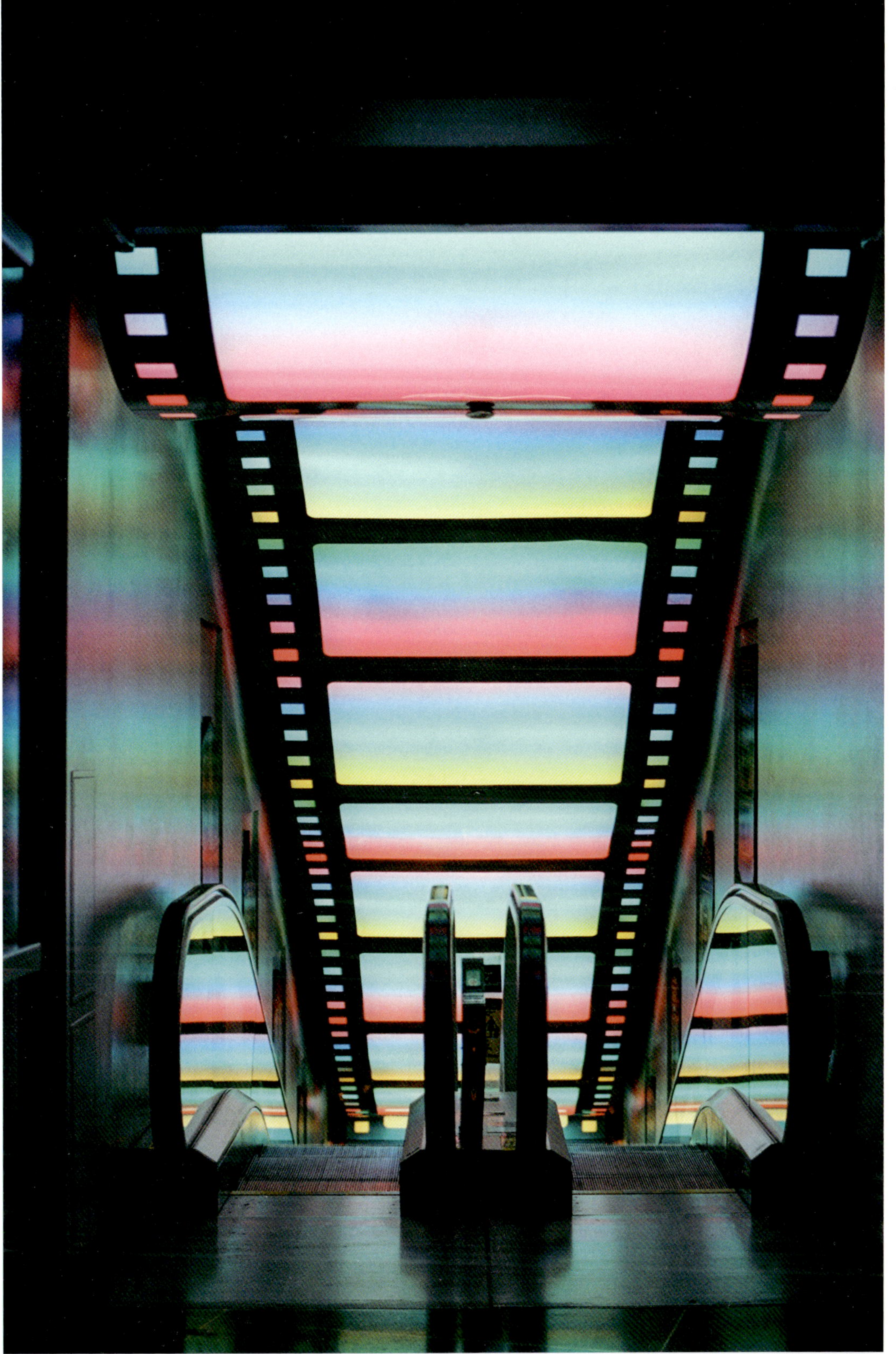

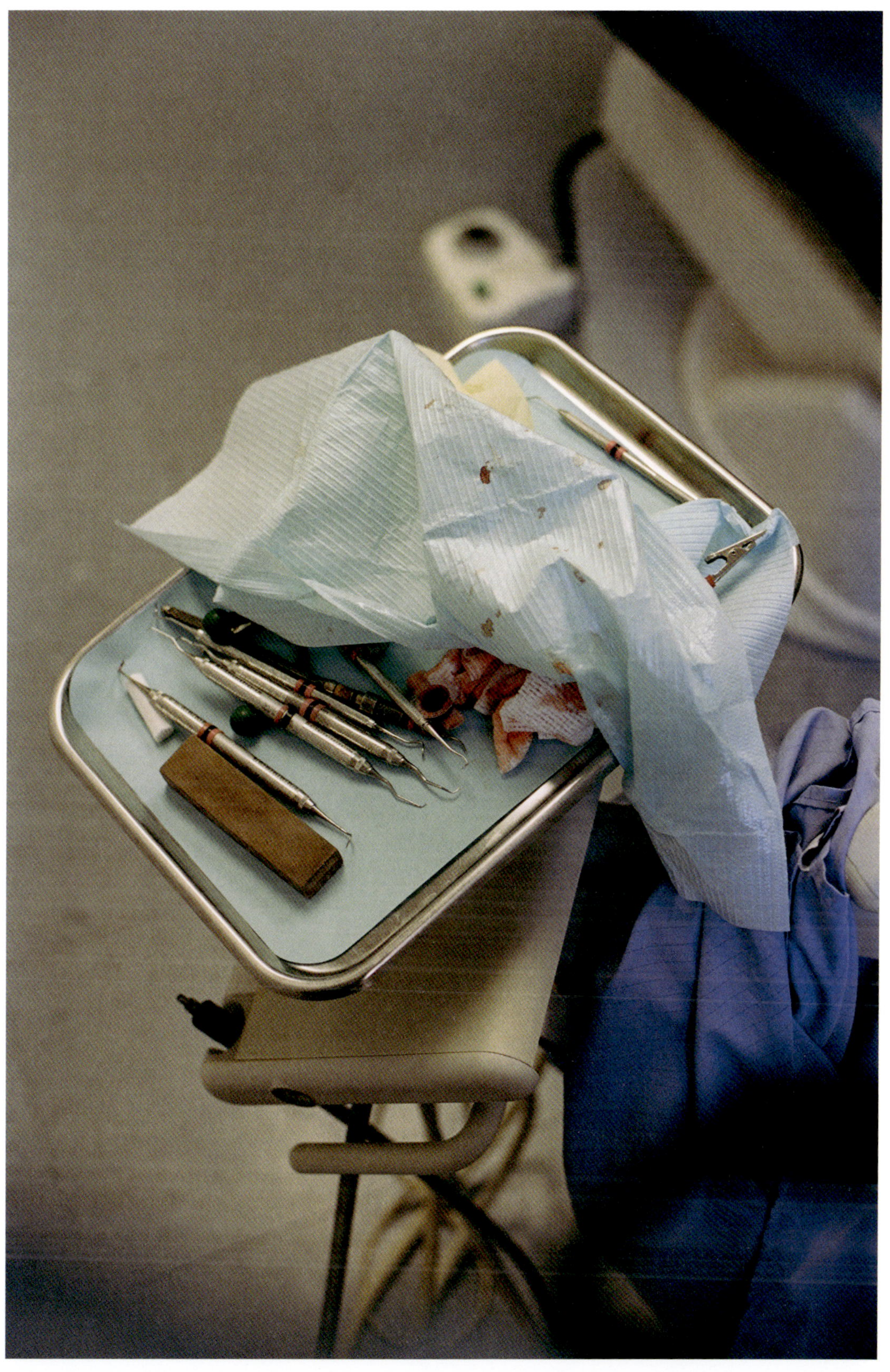

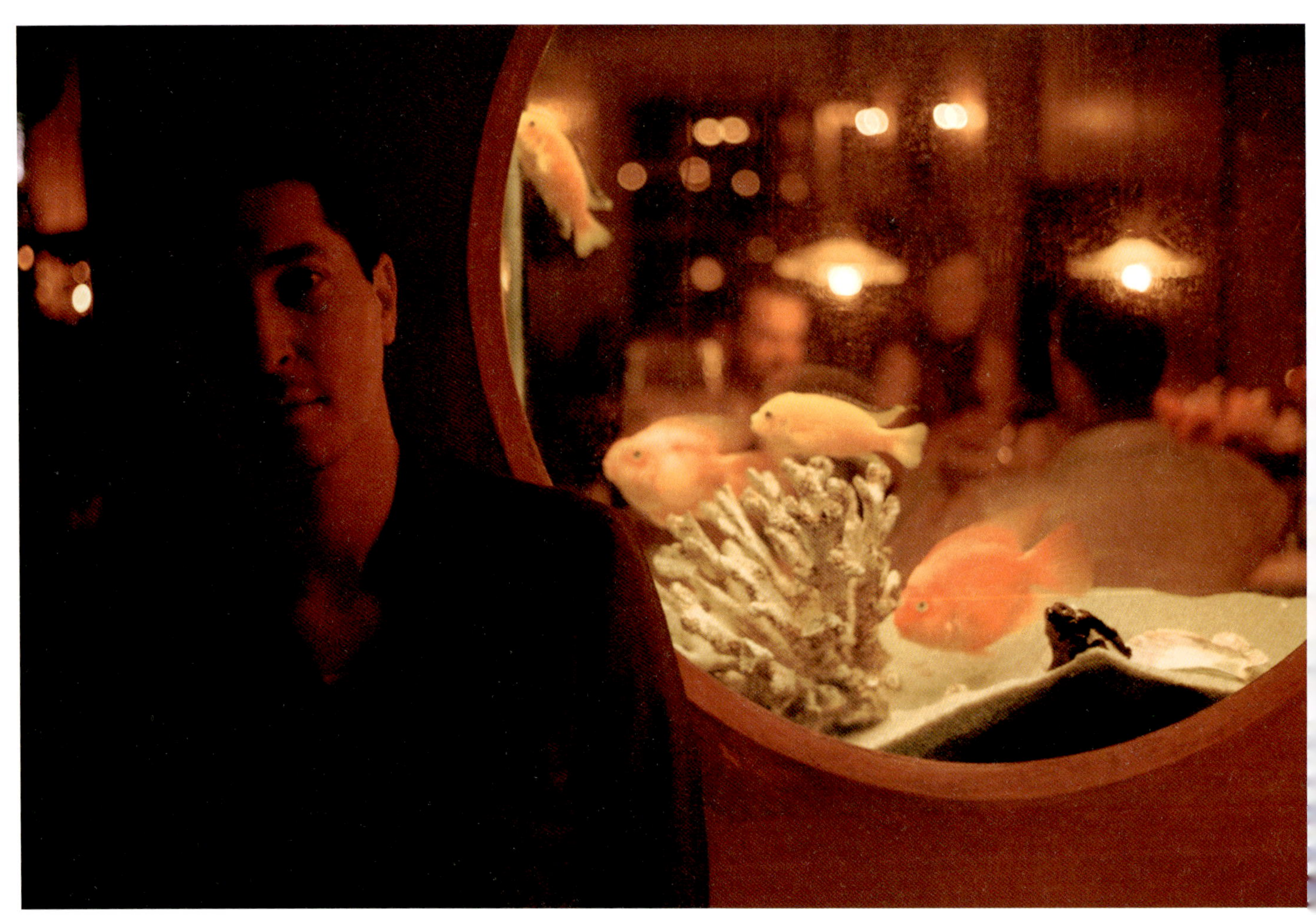

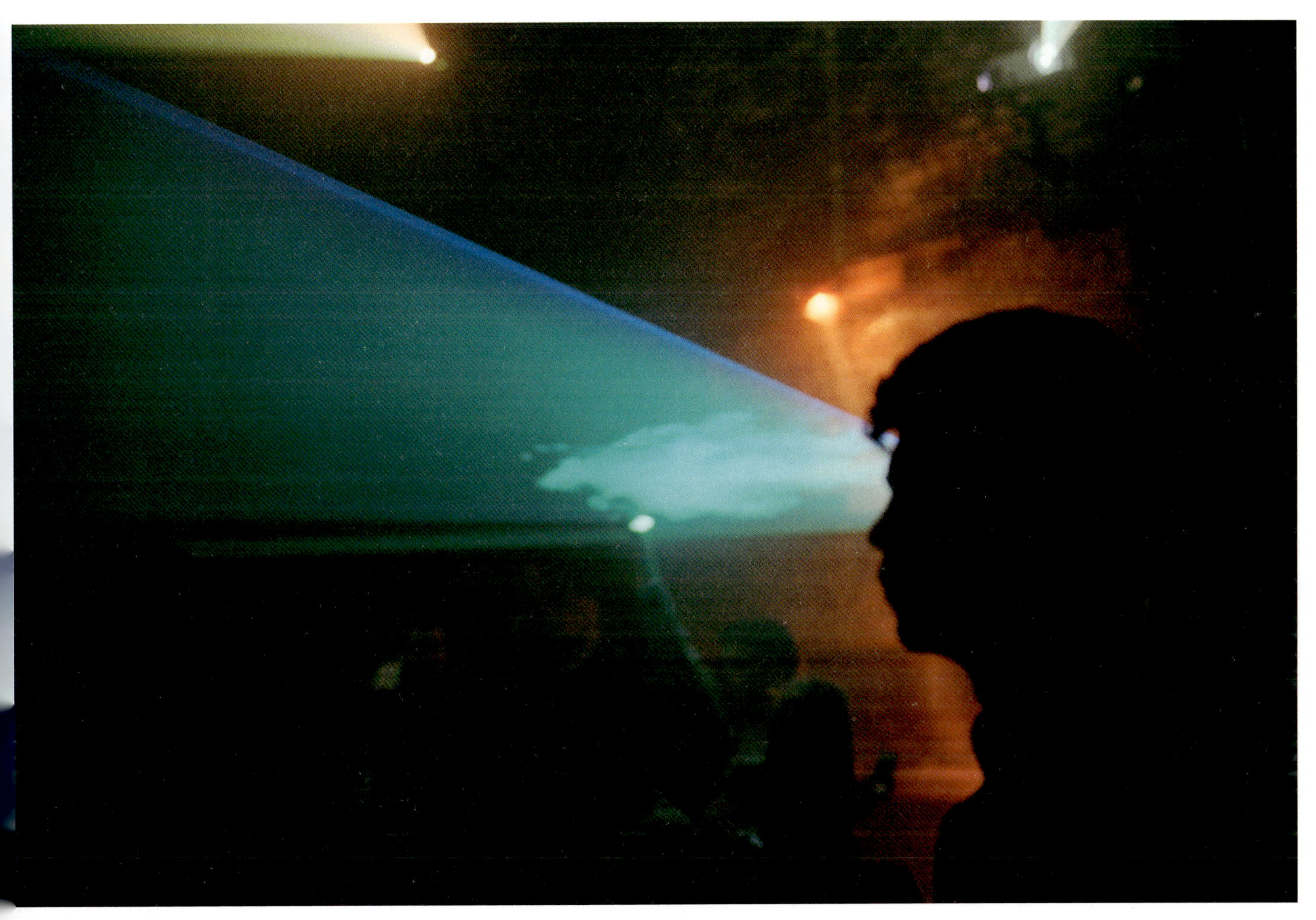

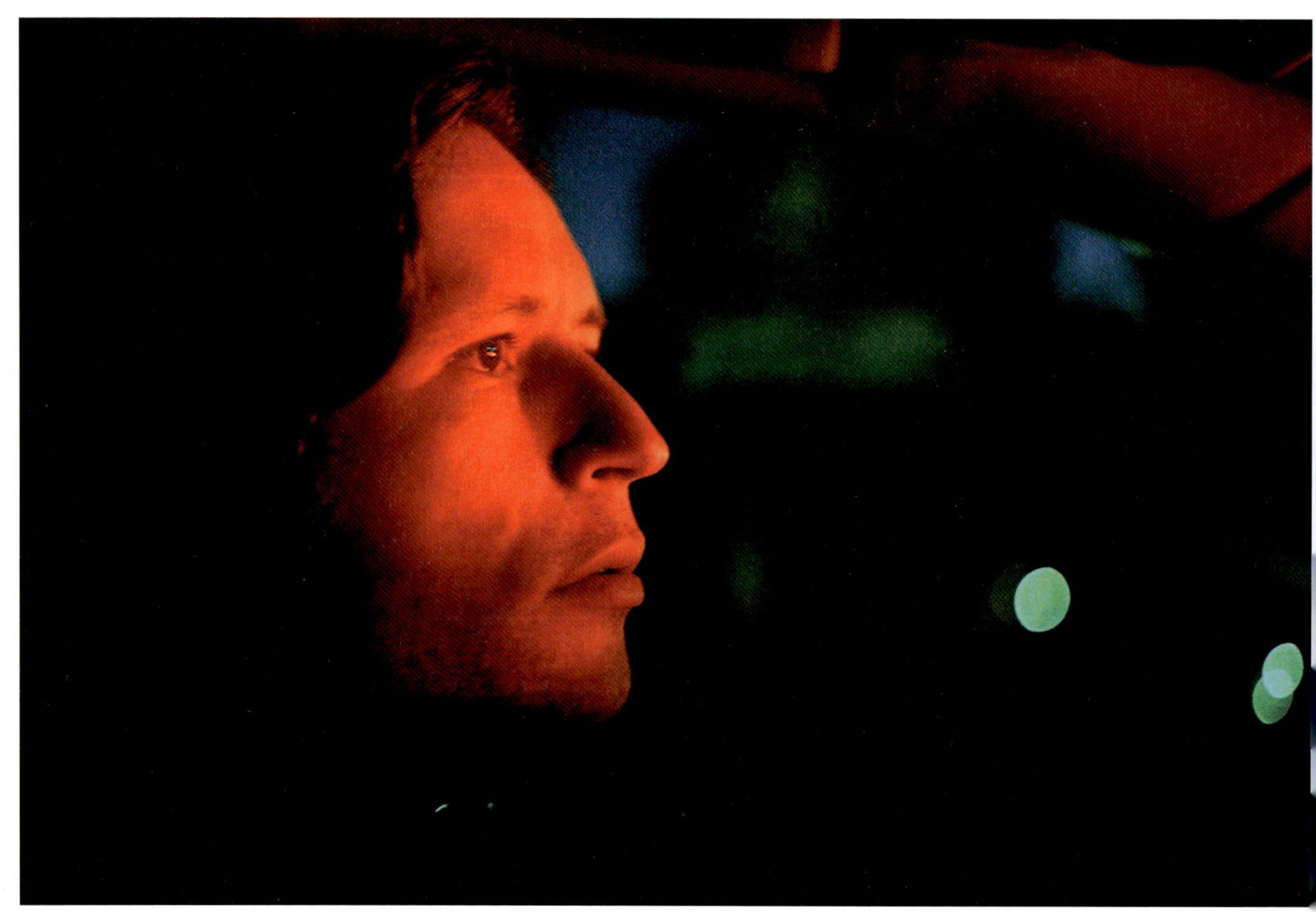

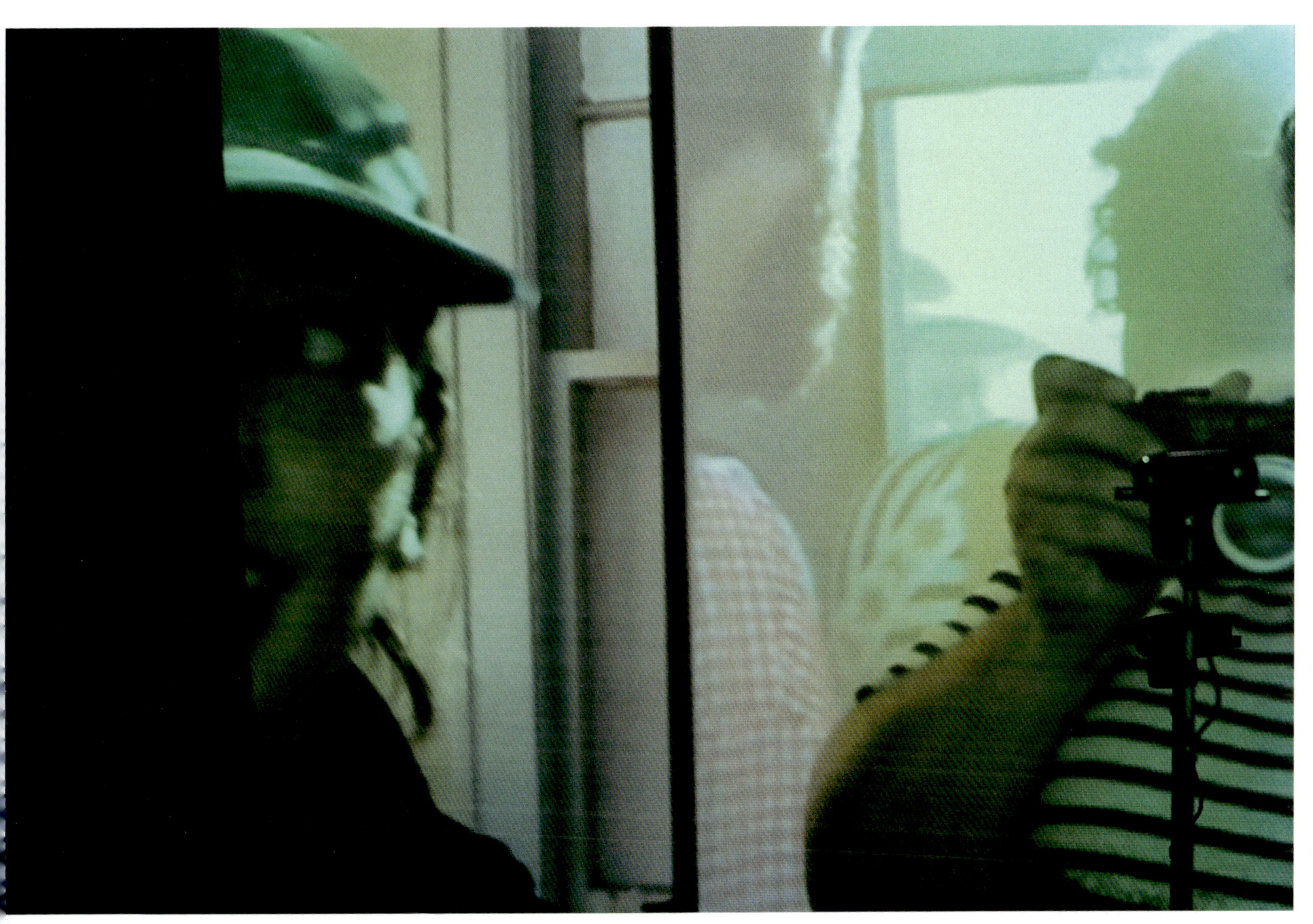

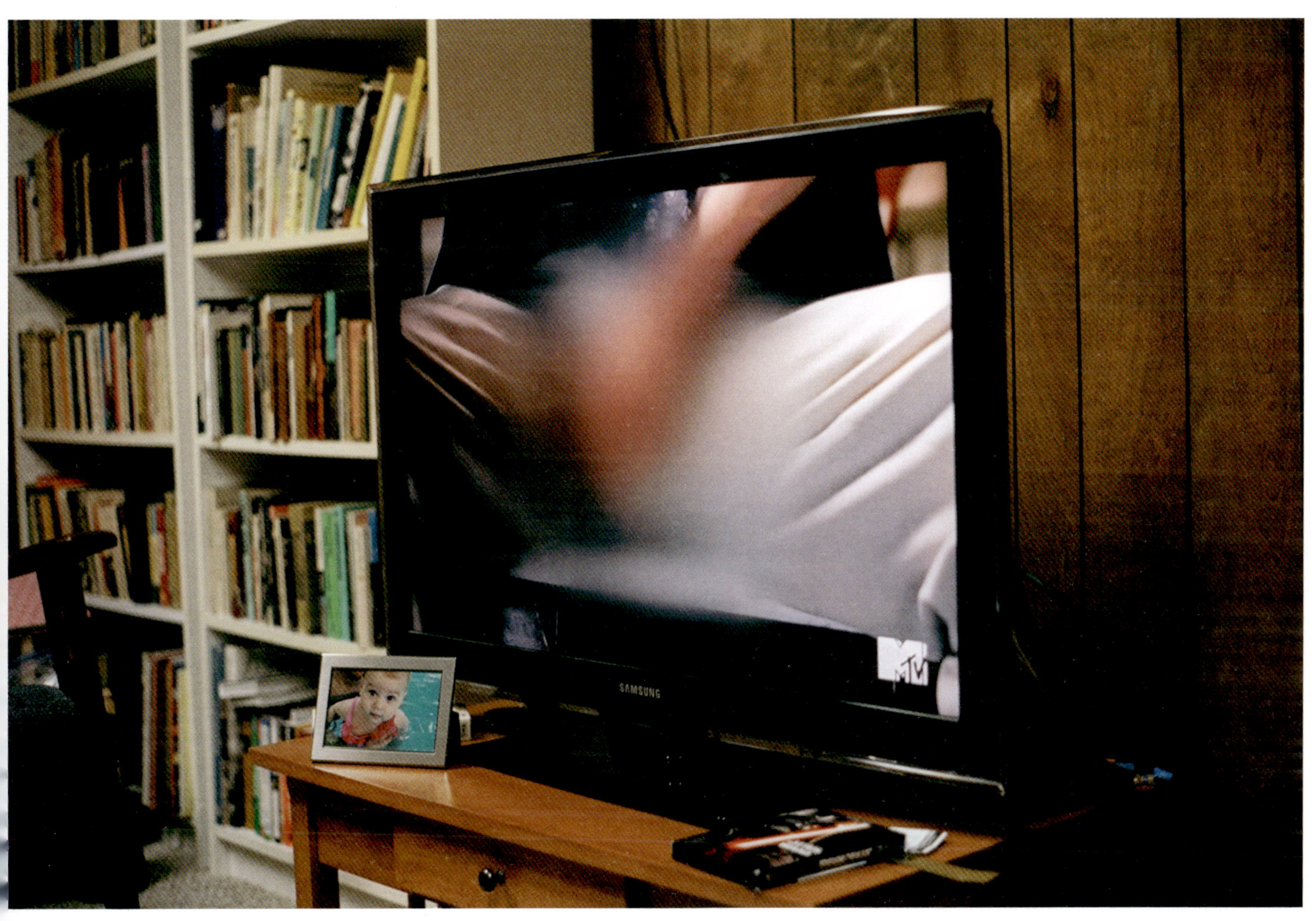

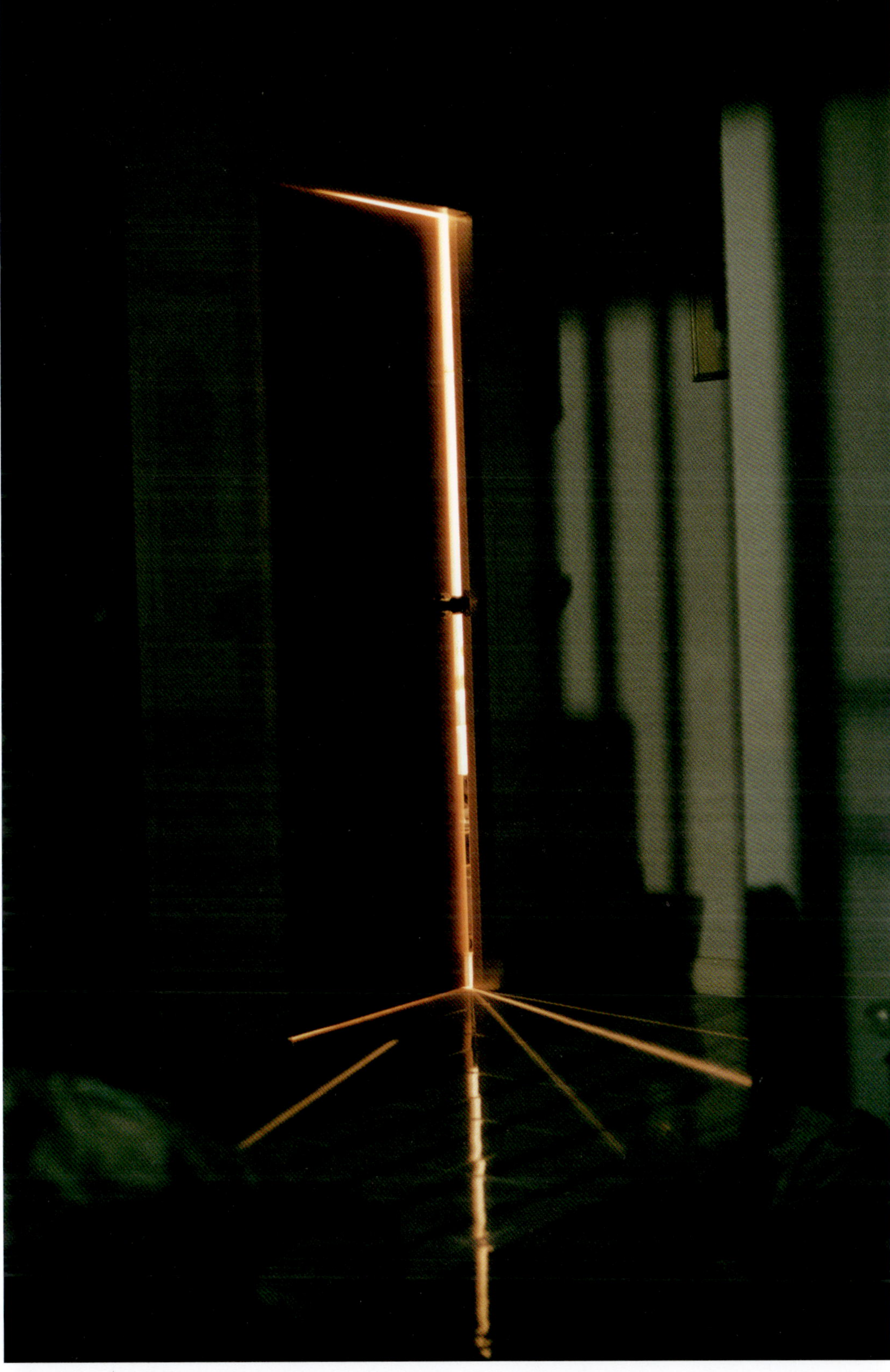

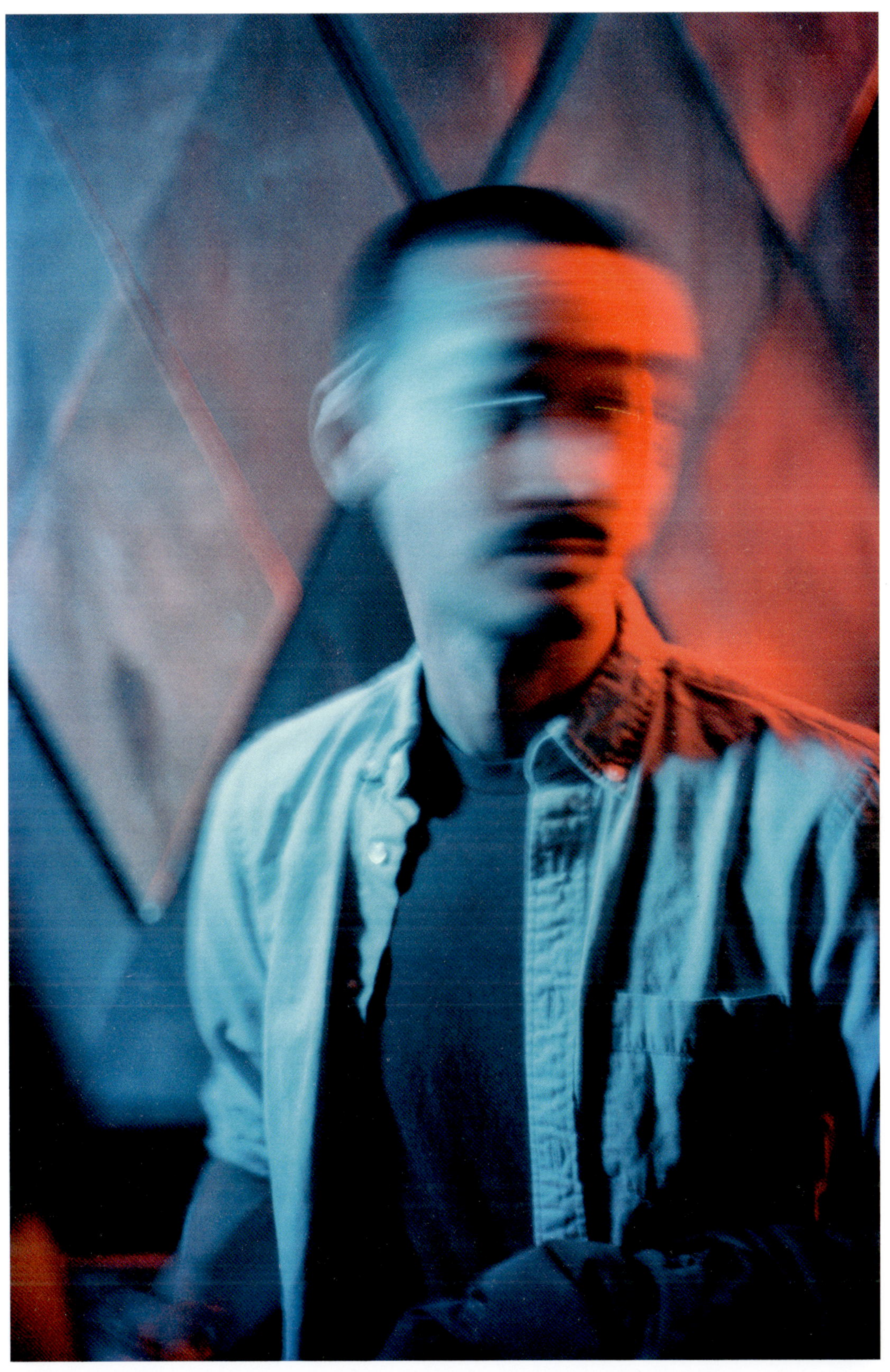

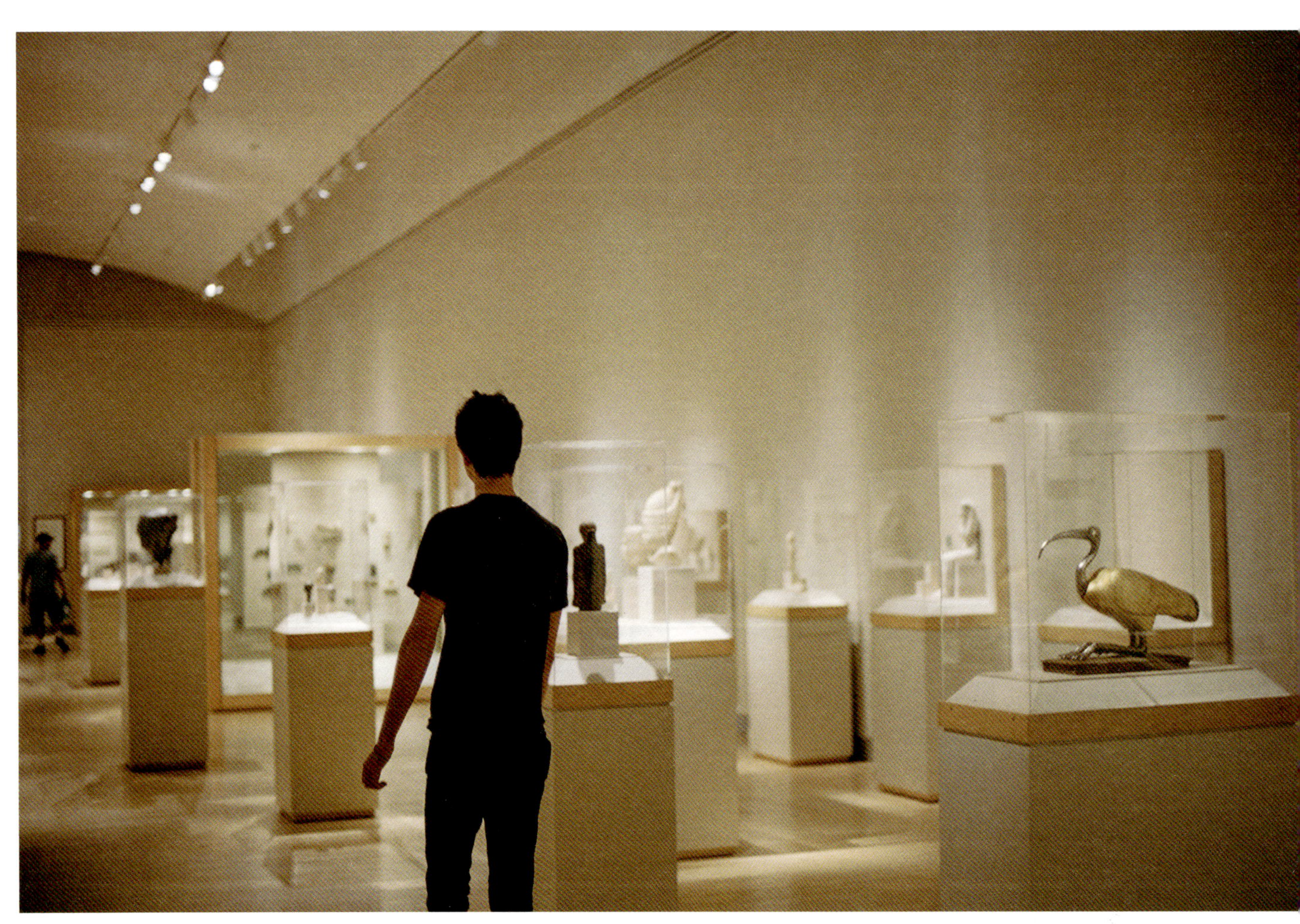

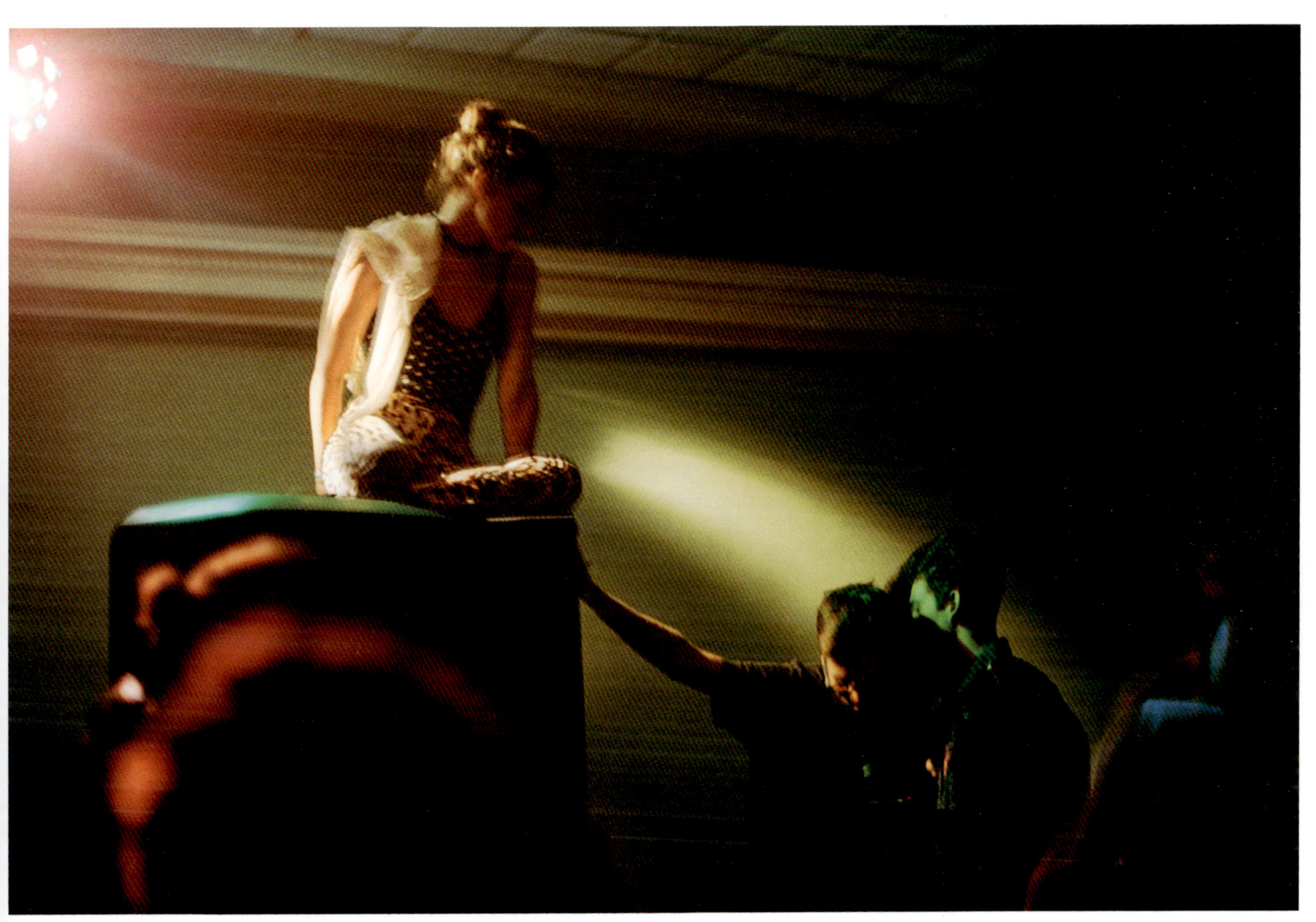

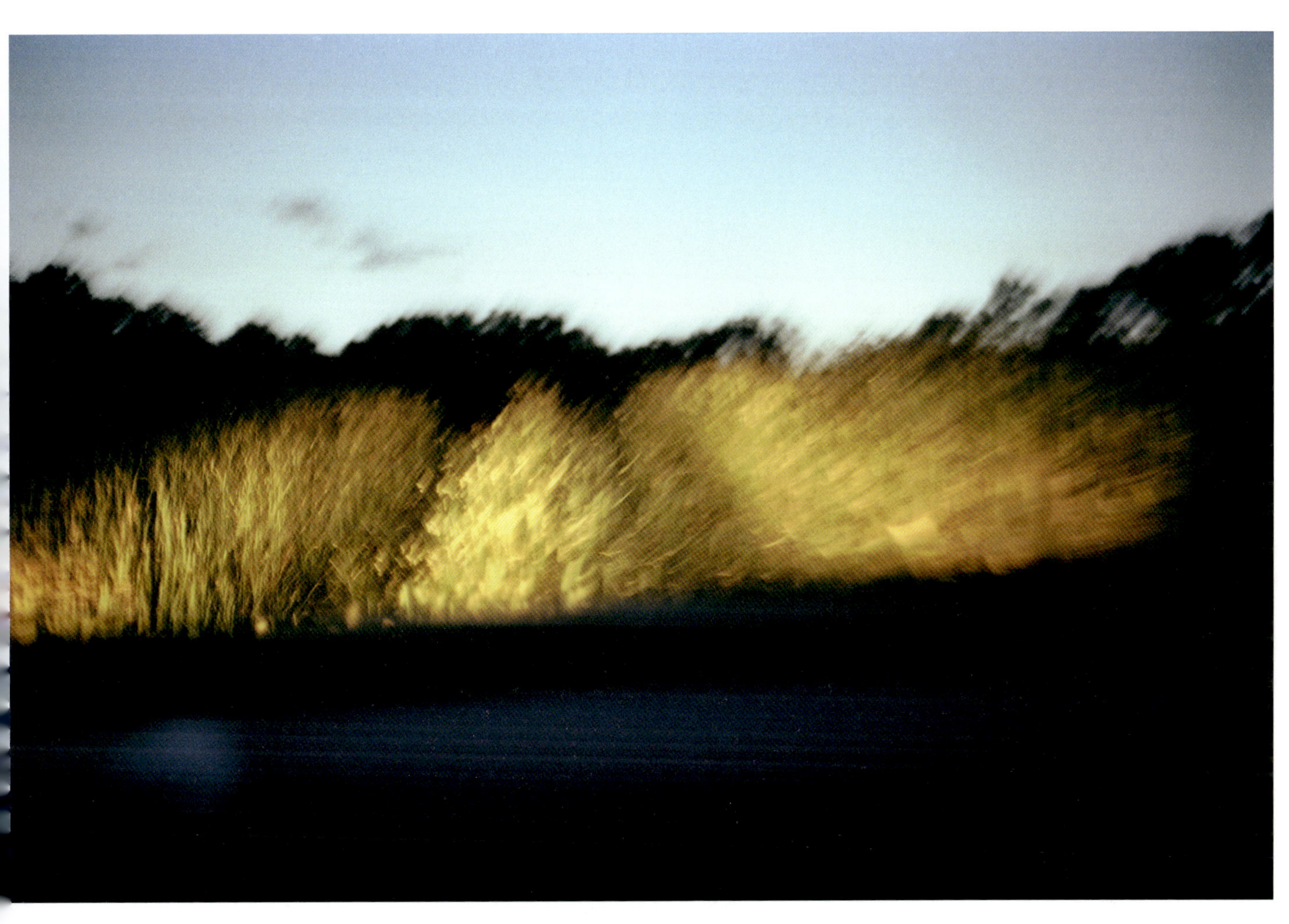

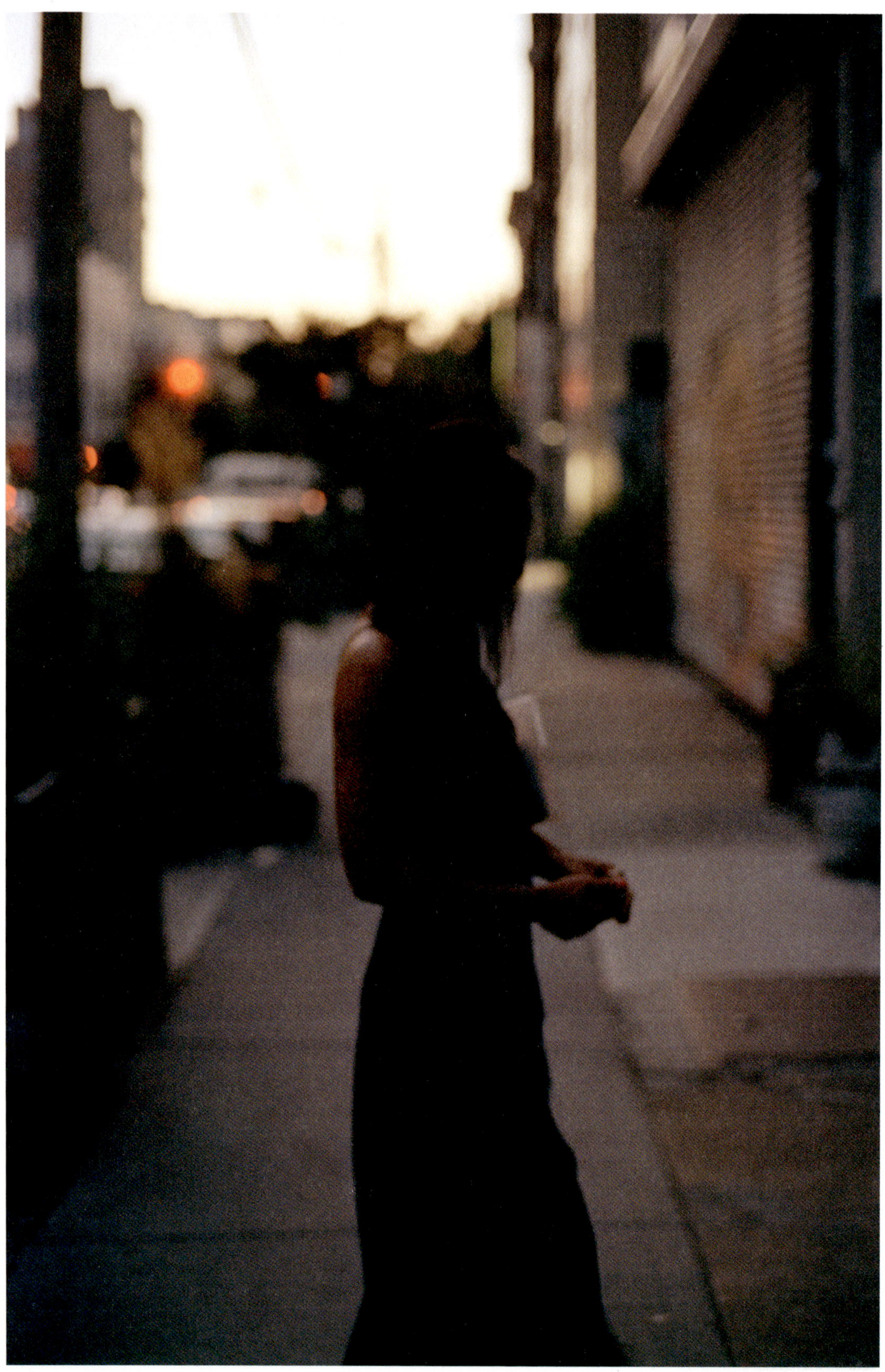

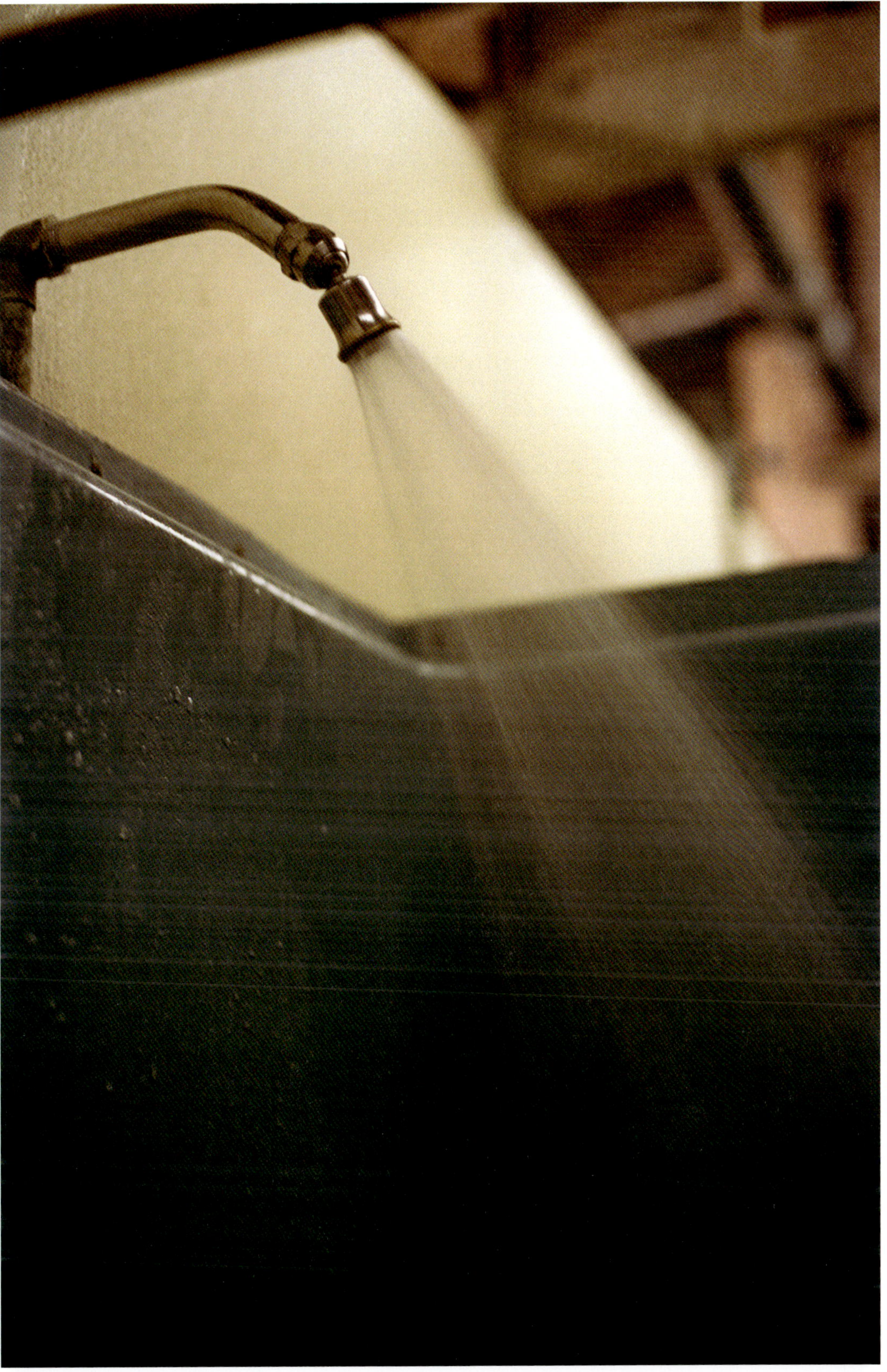

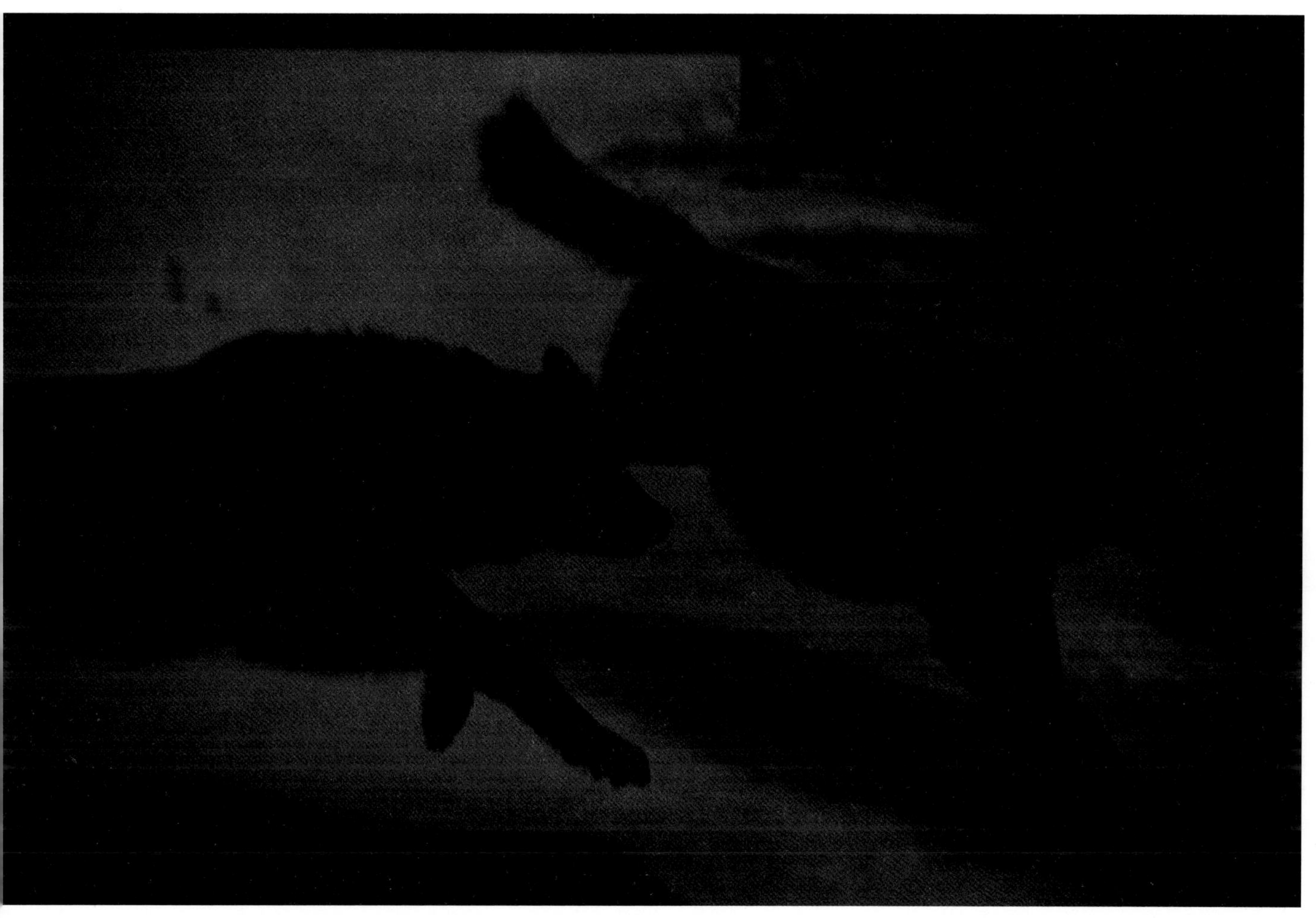

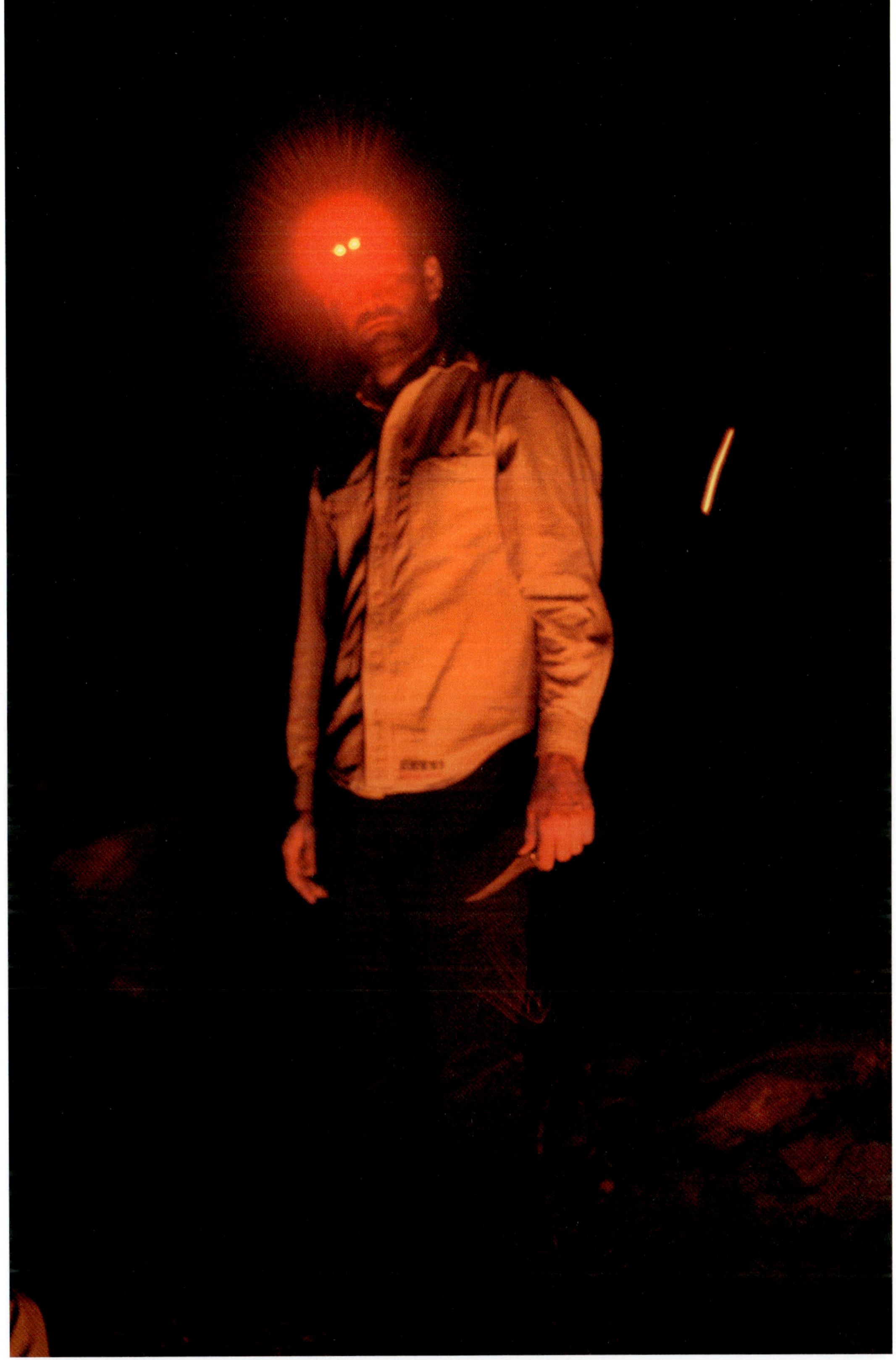

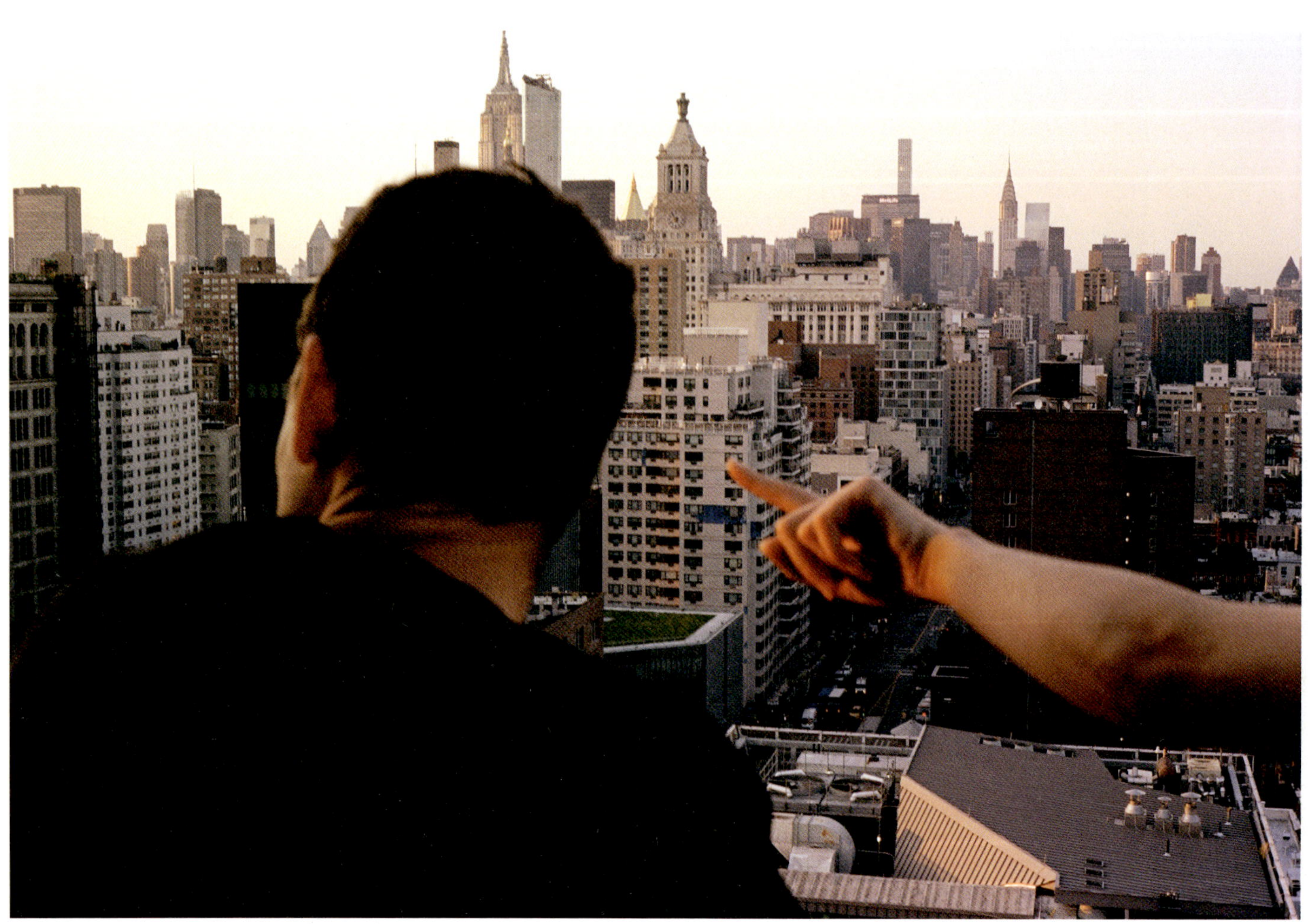

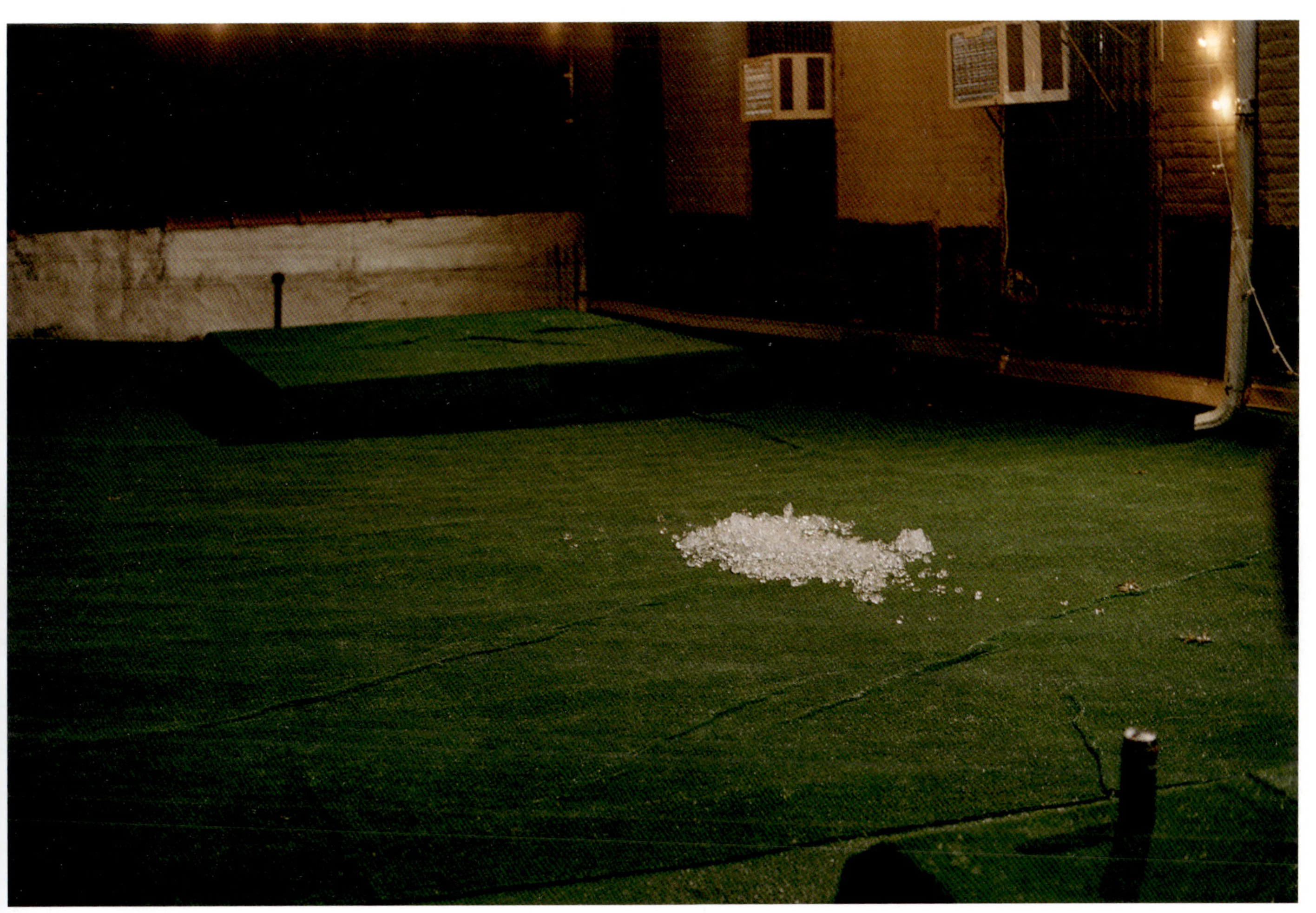

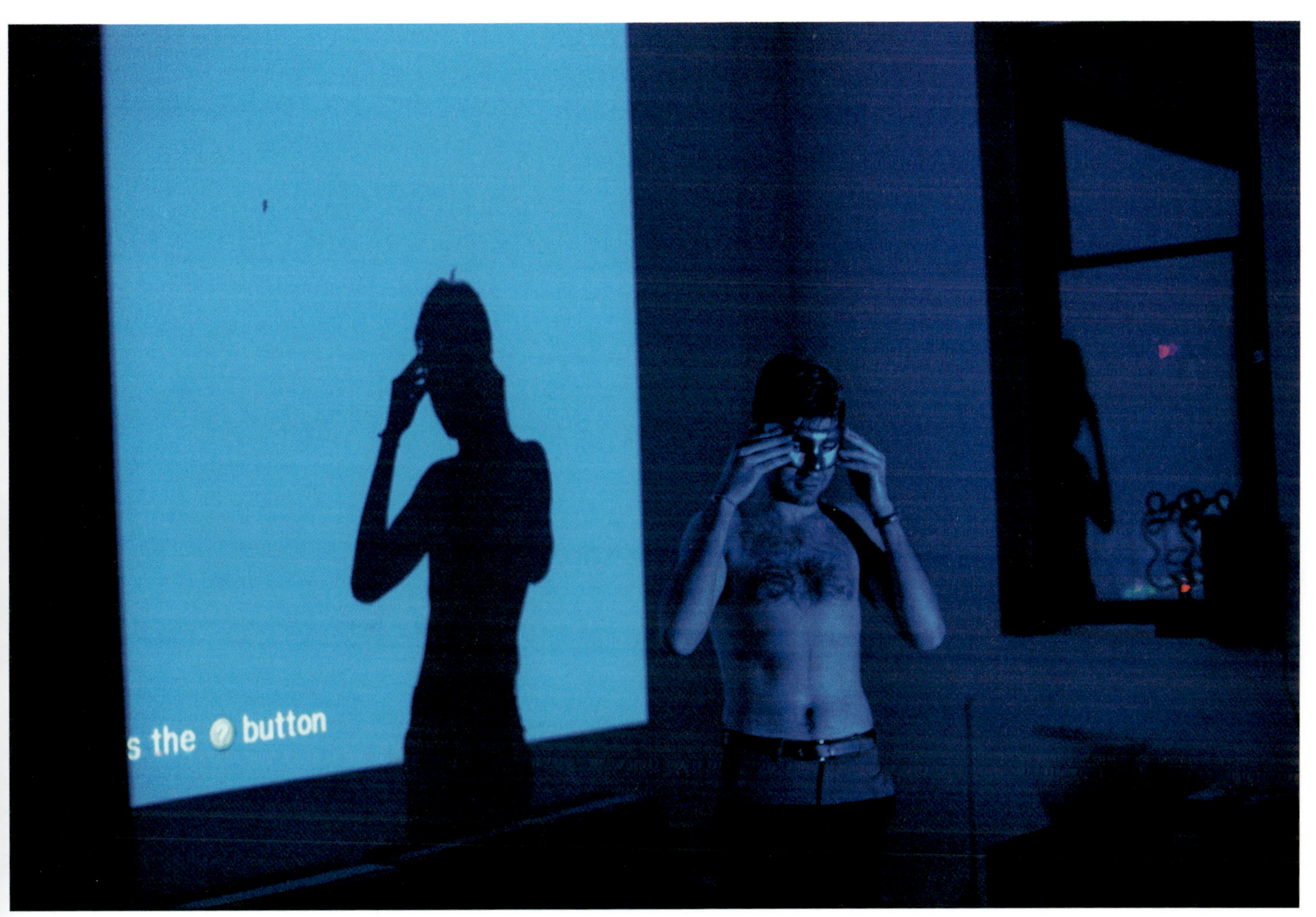
s the ? button

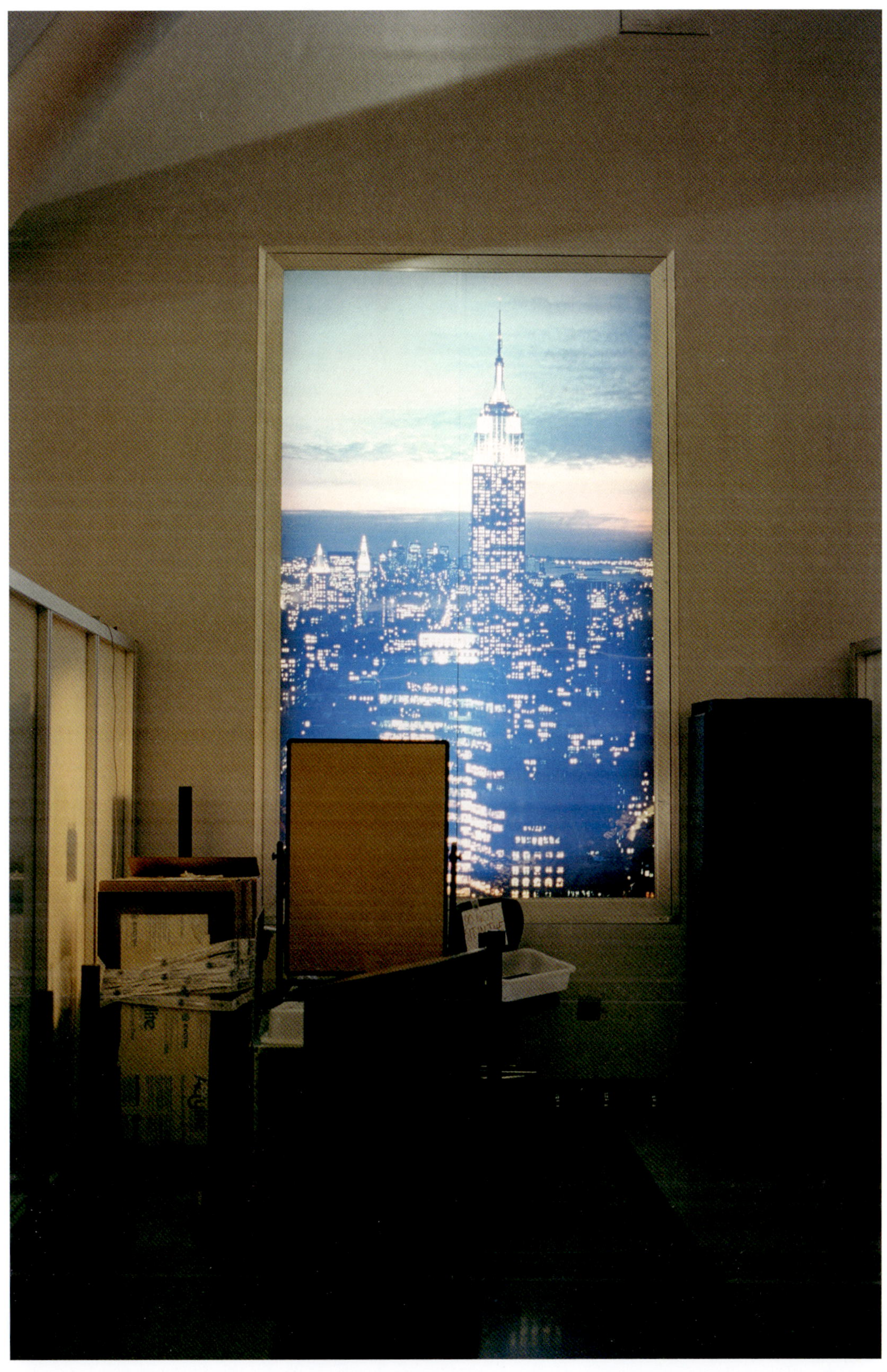

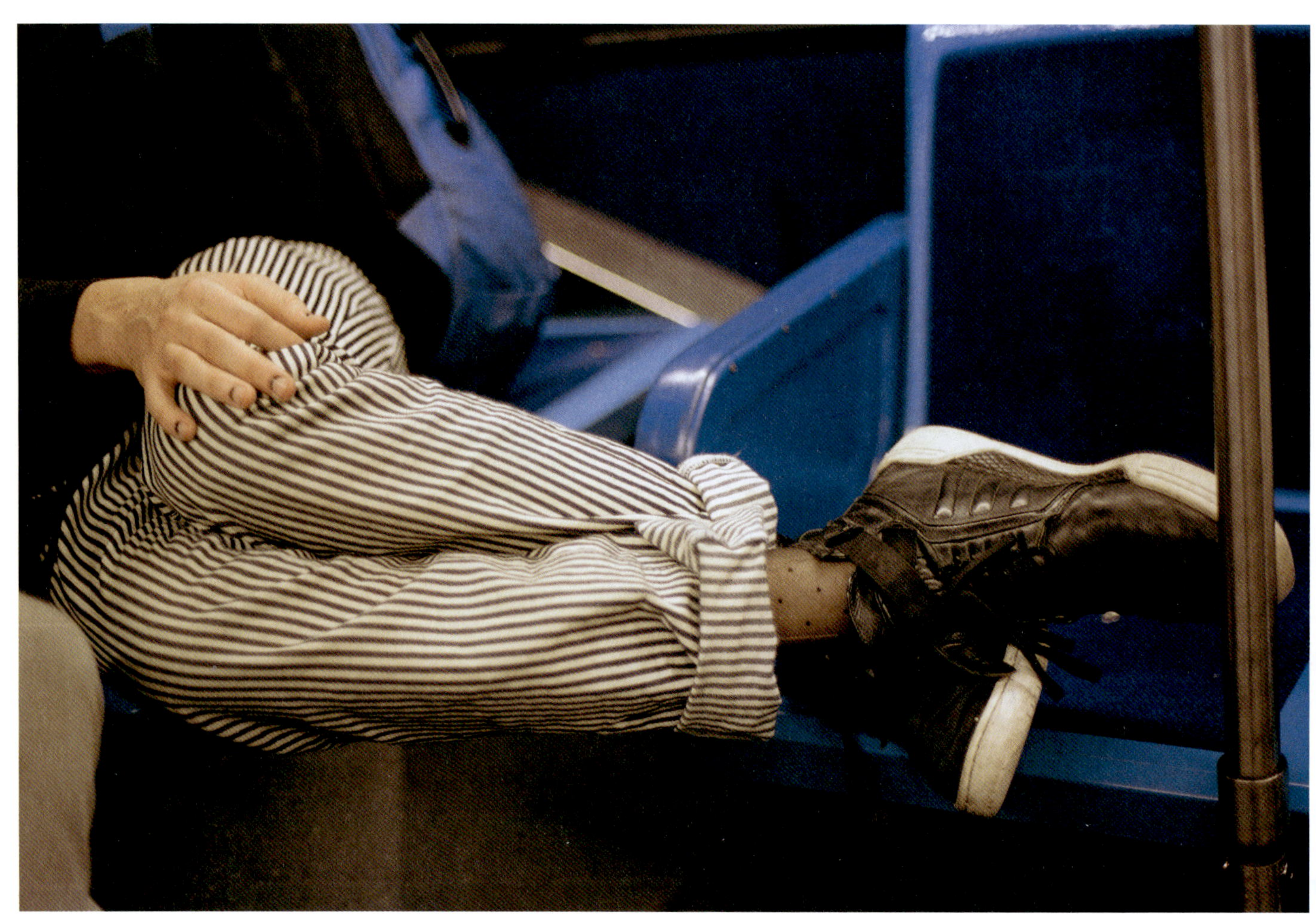

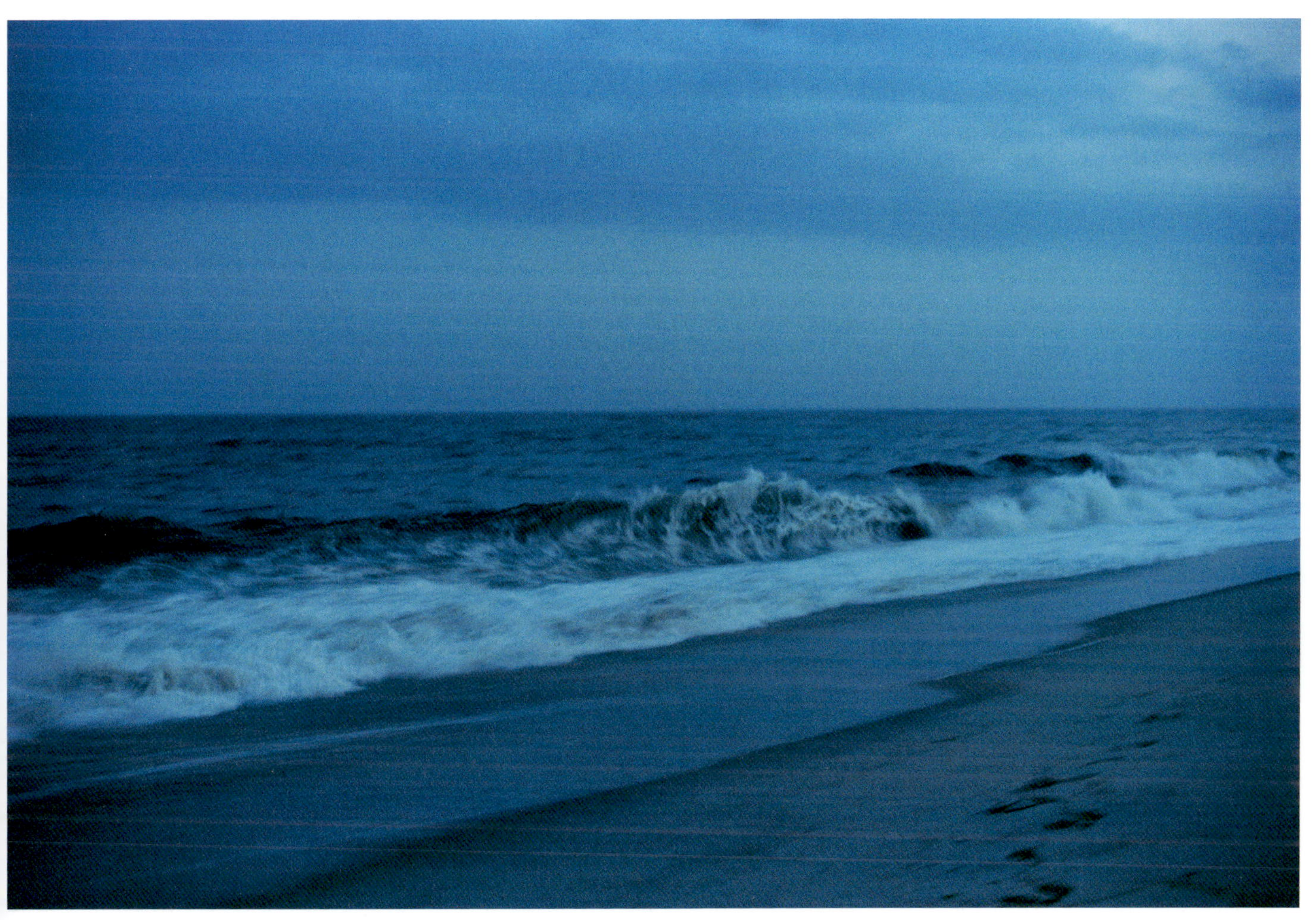

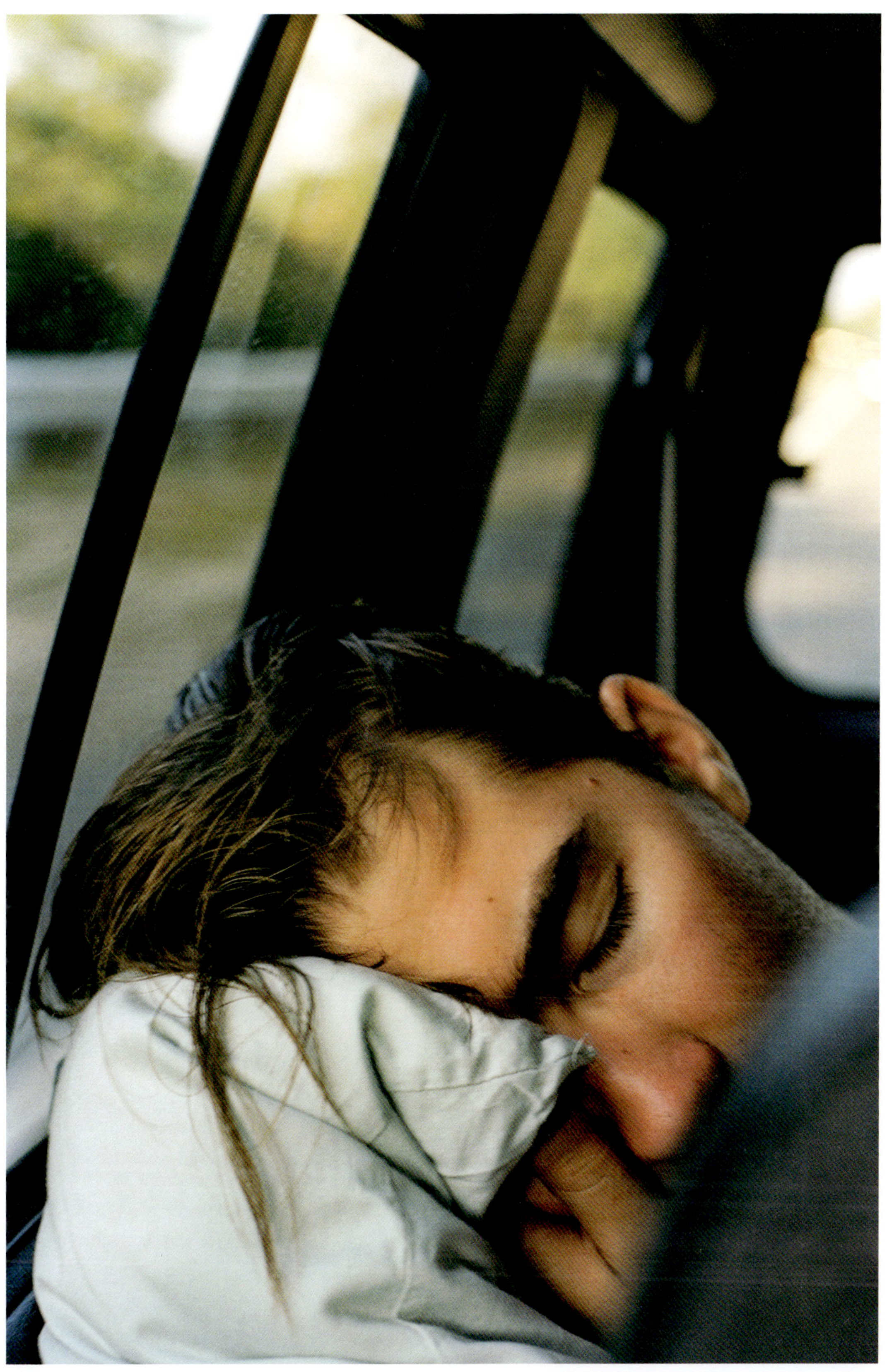

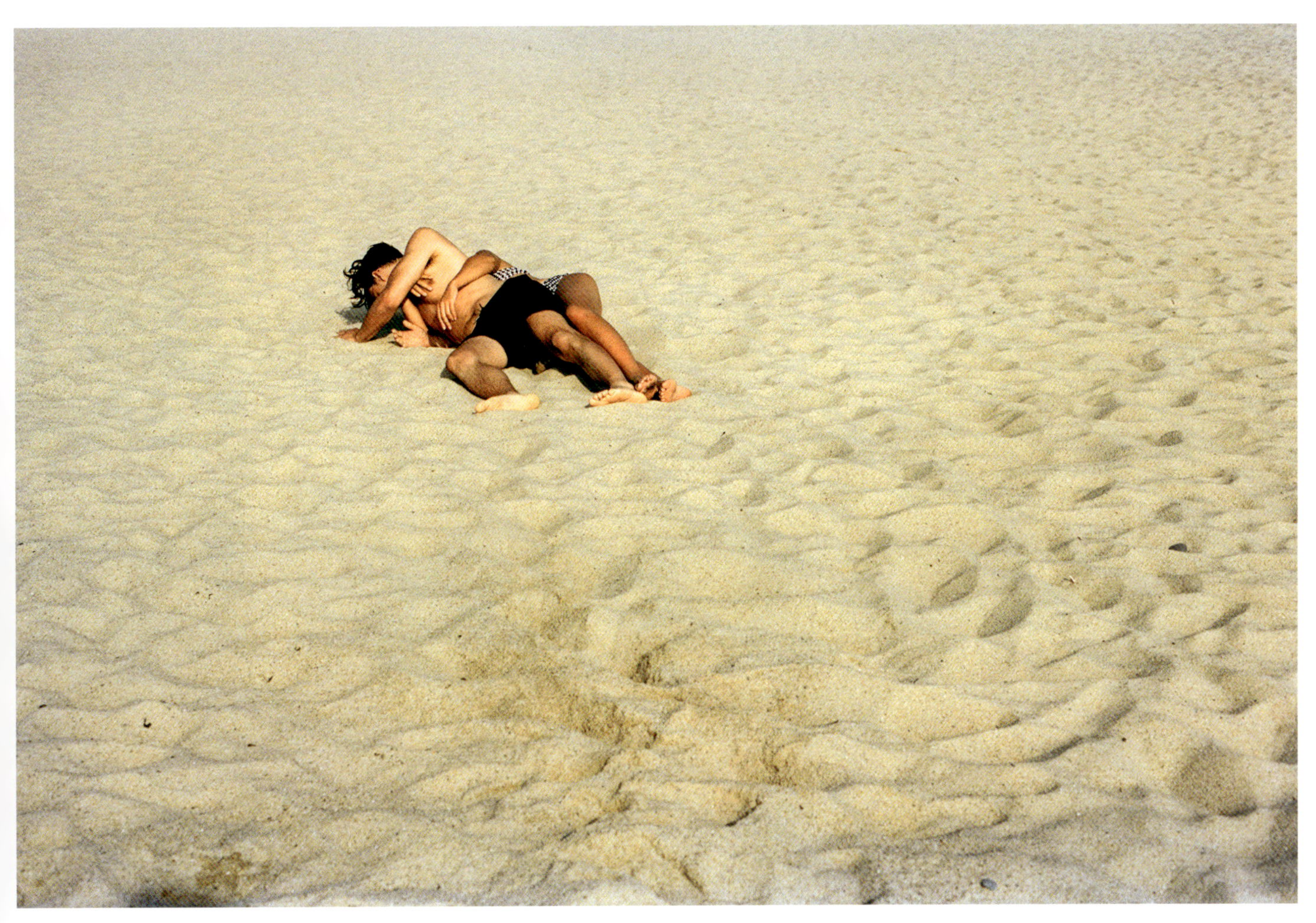

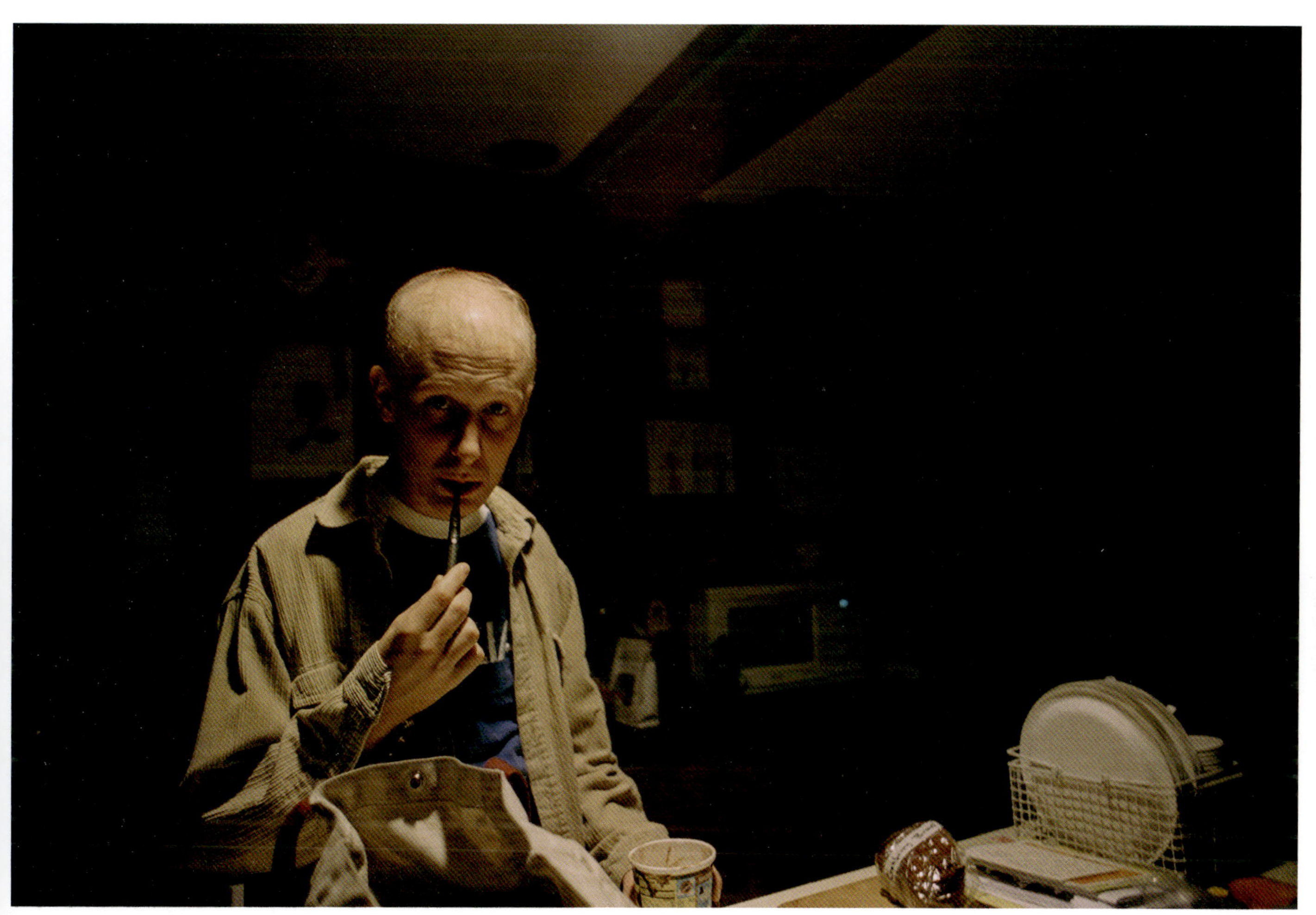

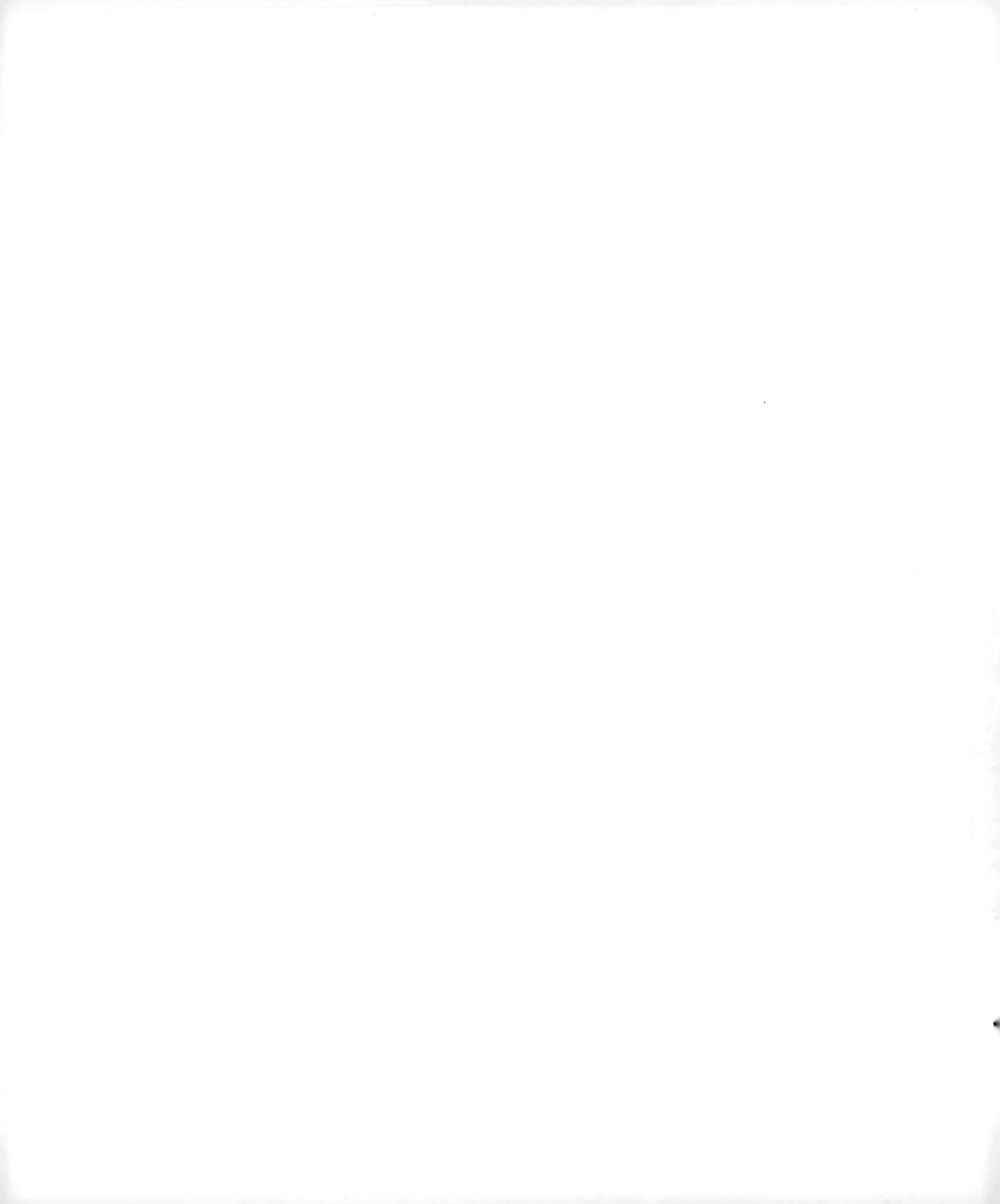

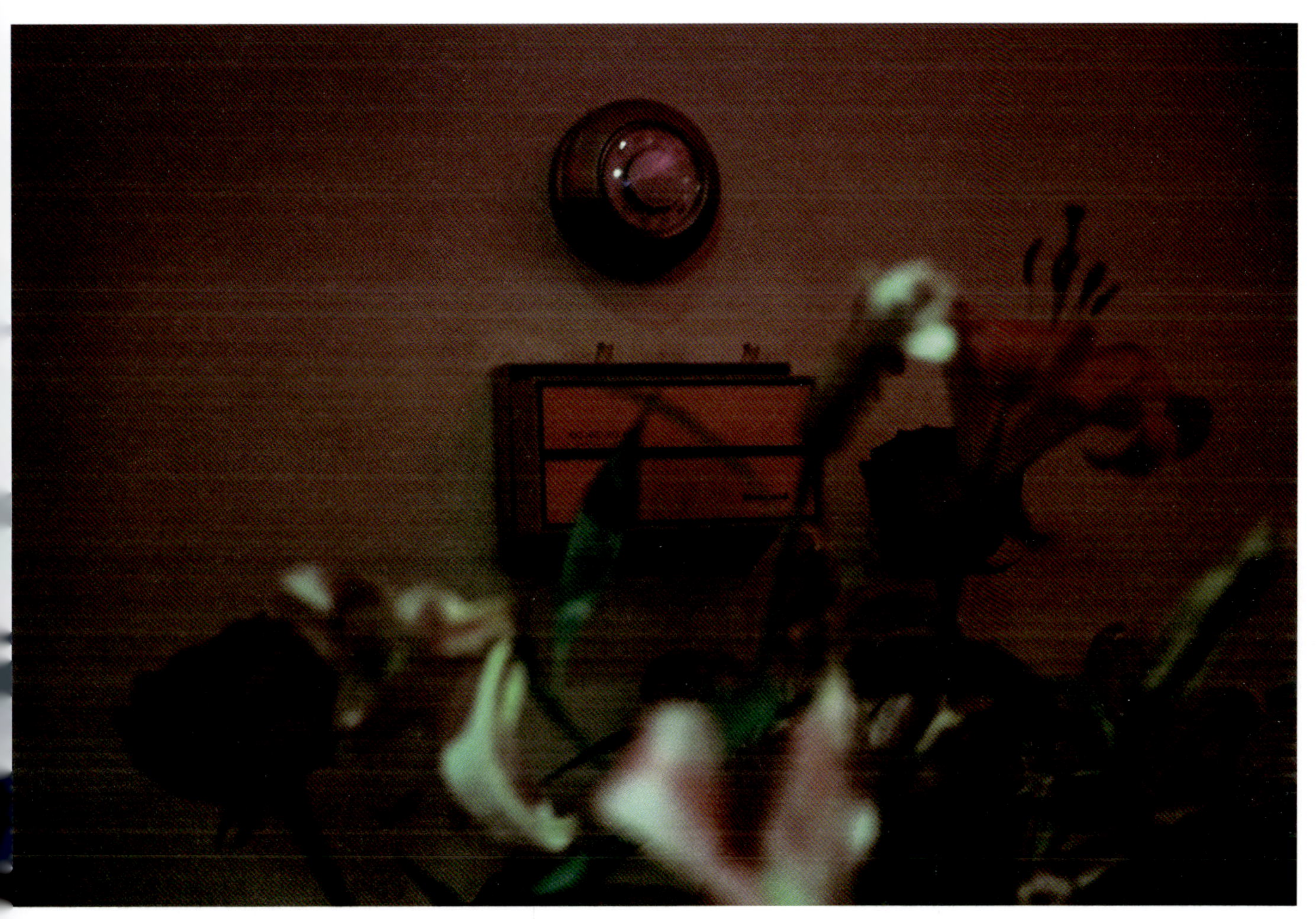

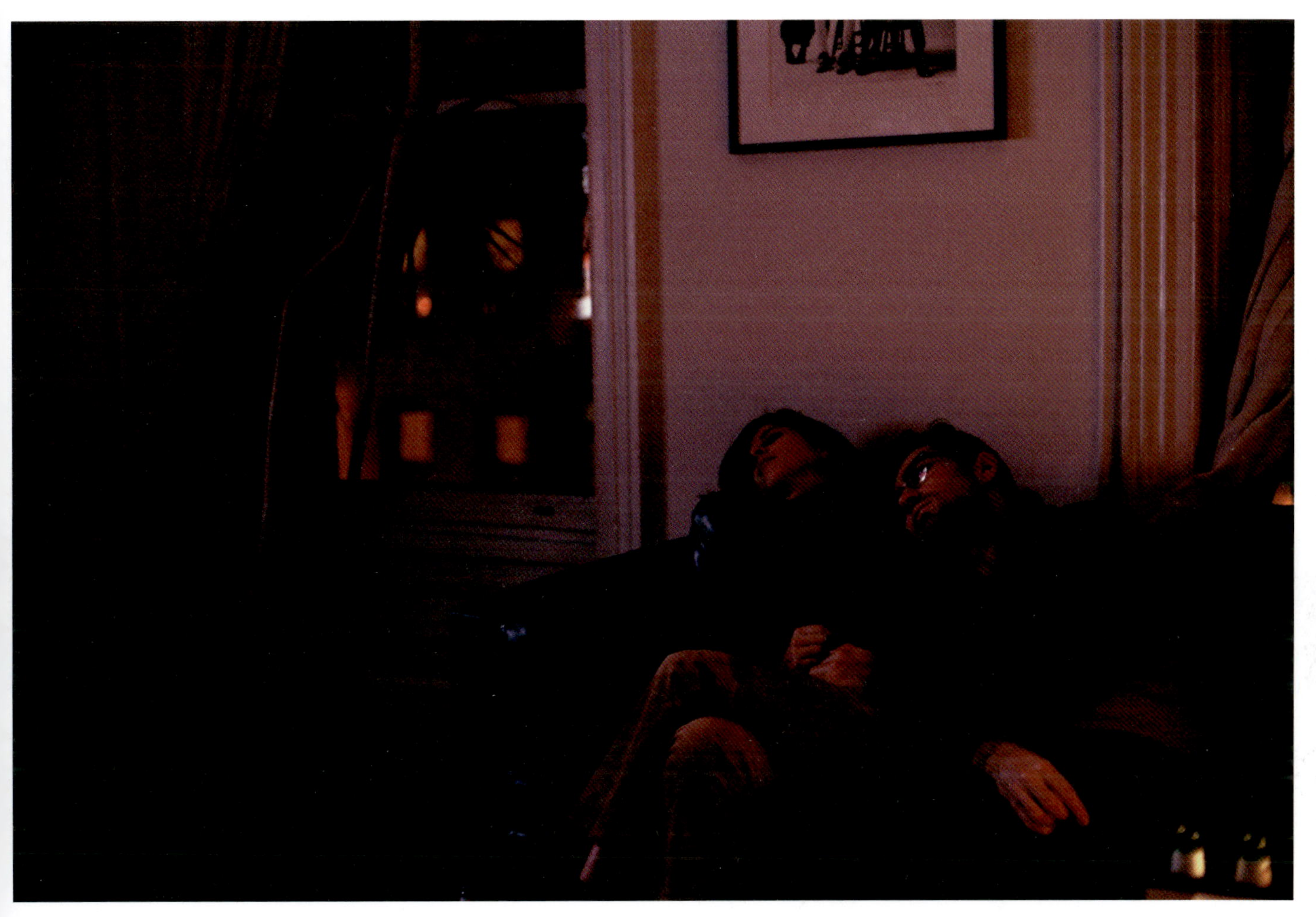

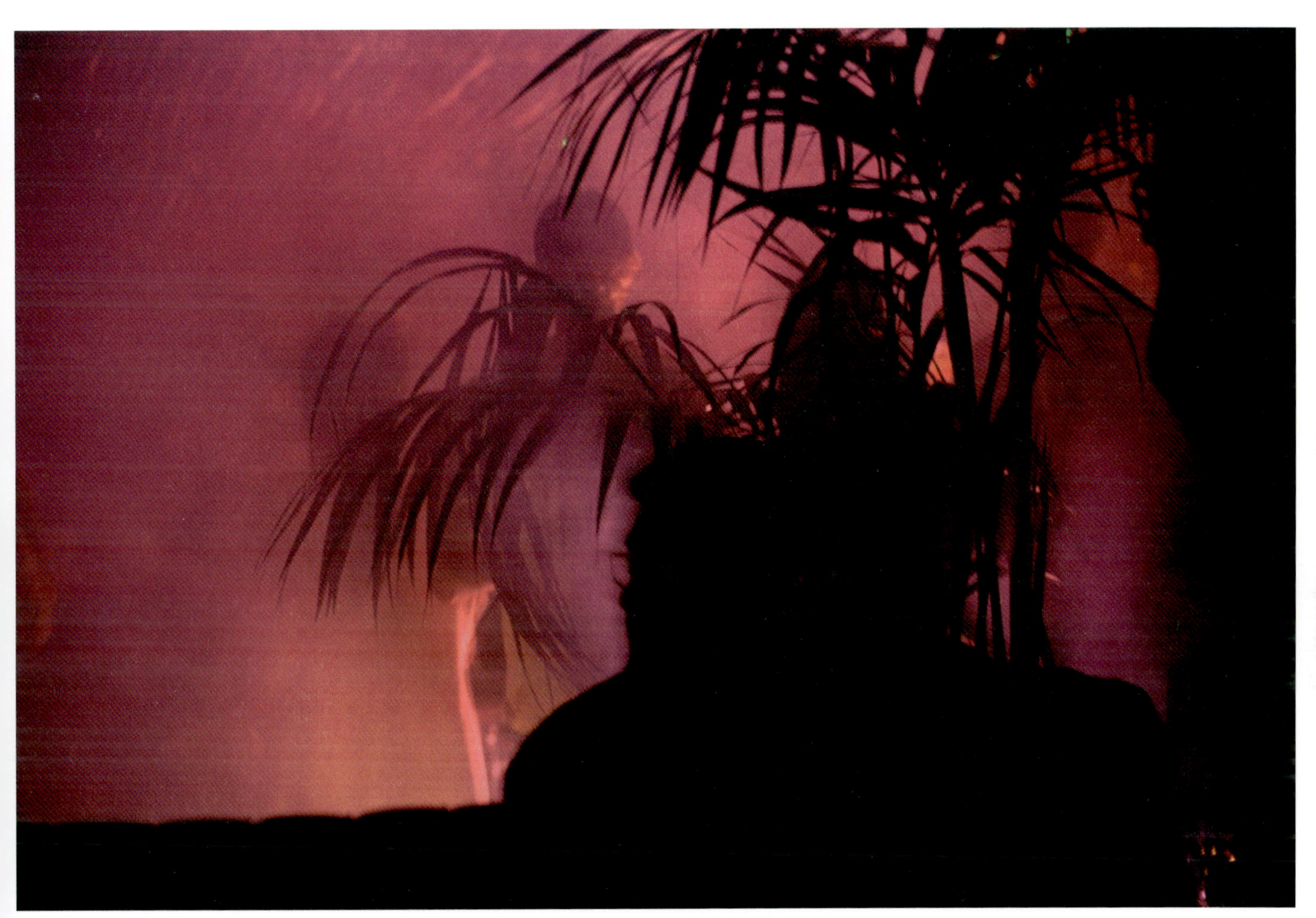

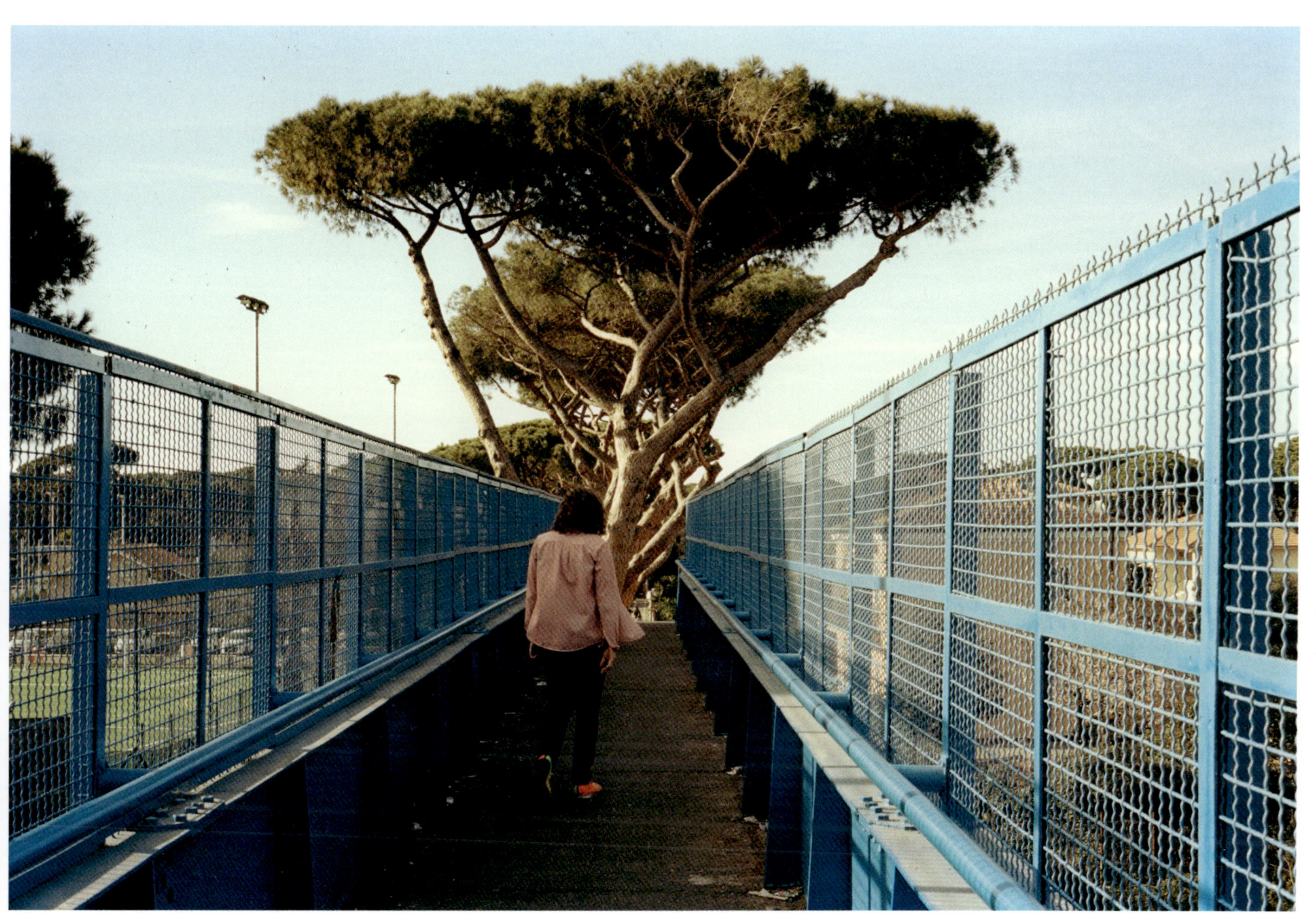

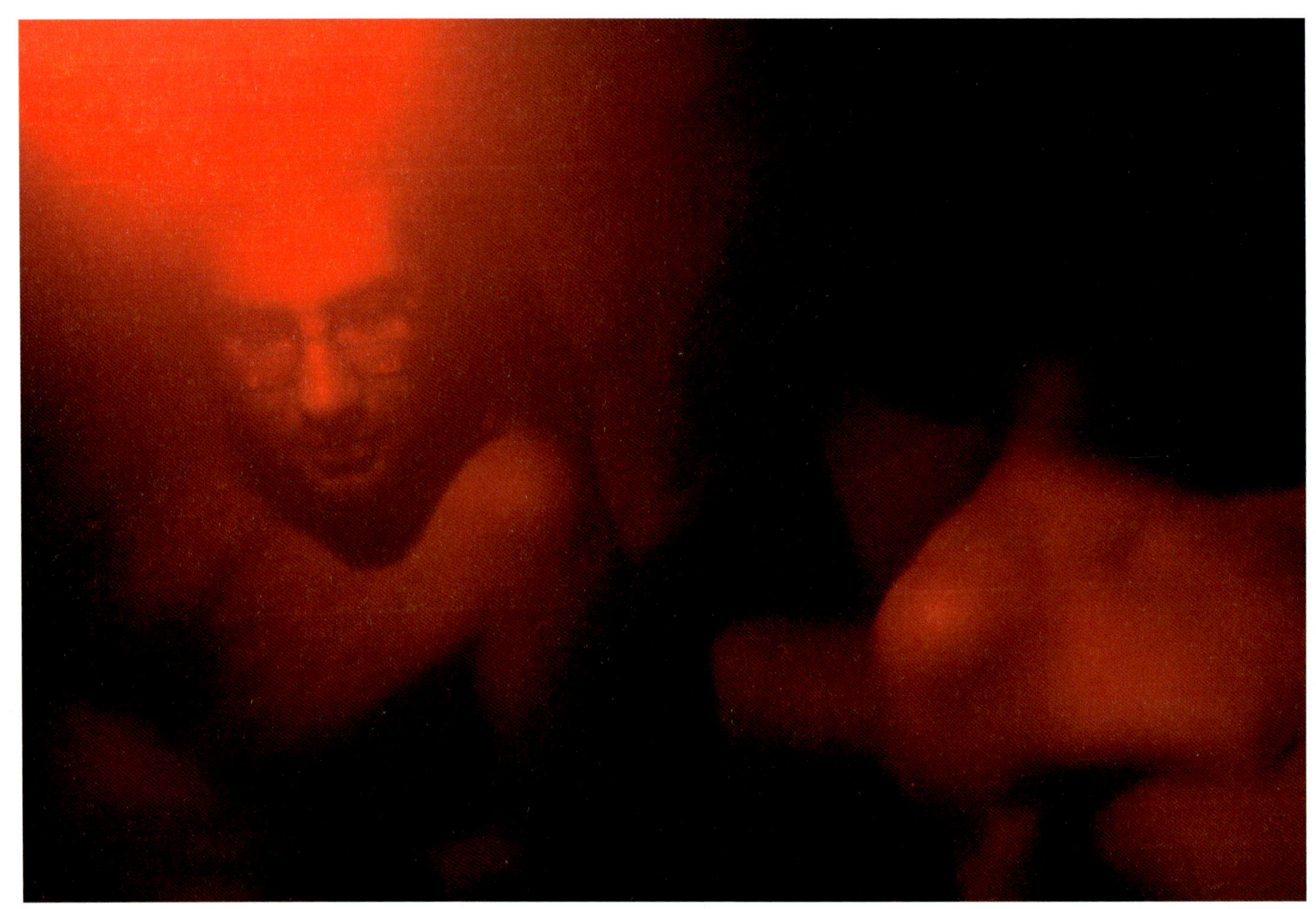

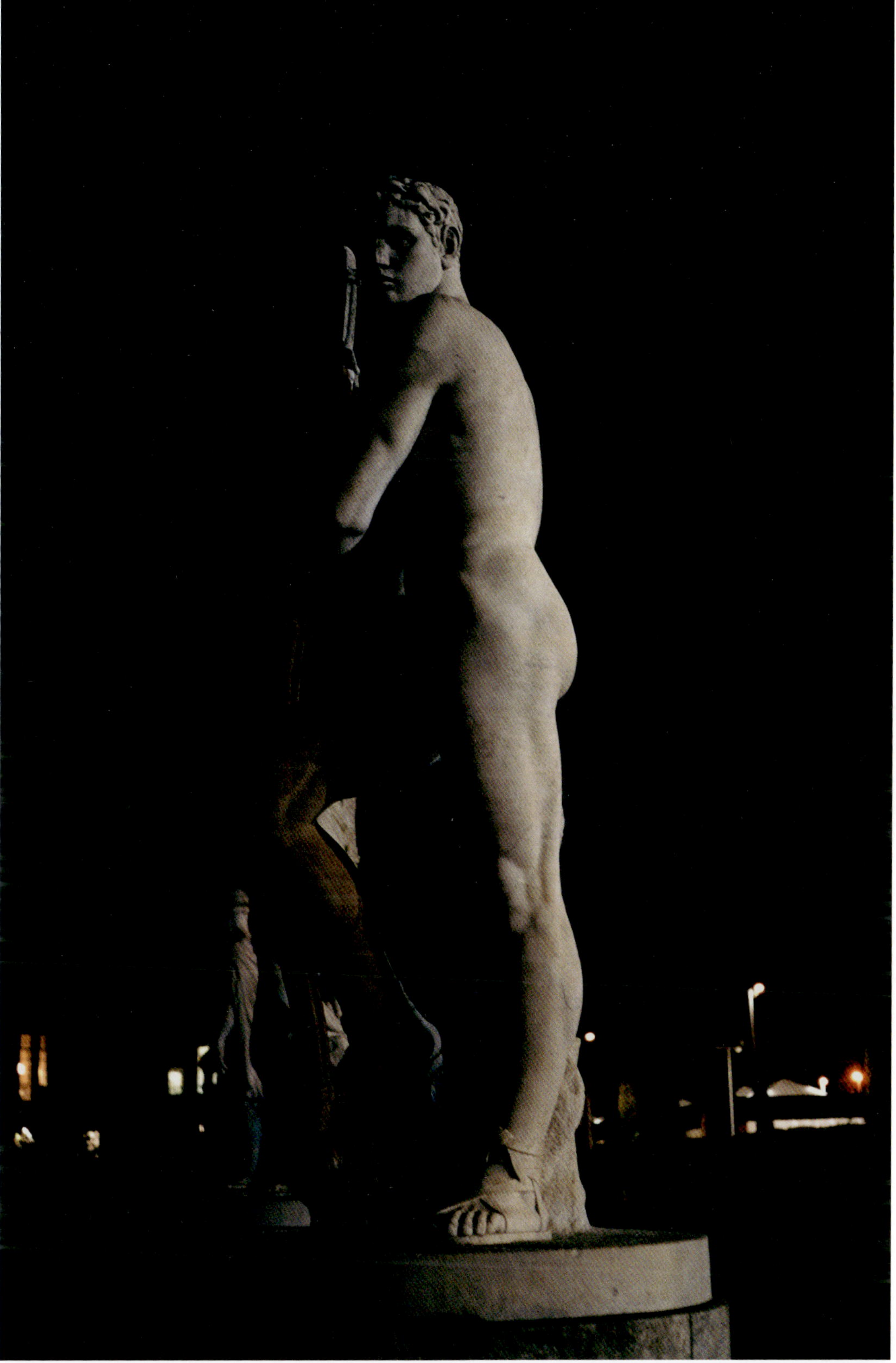

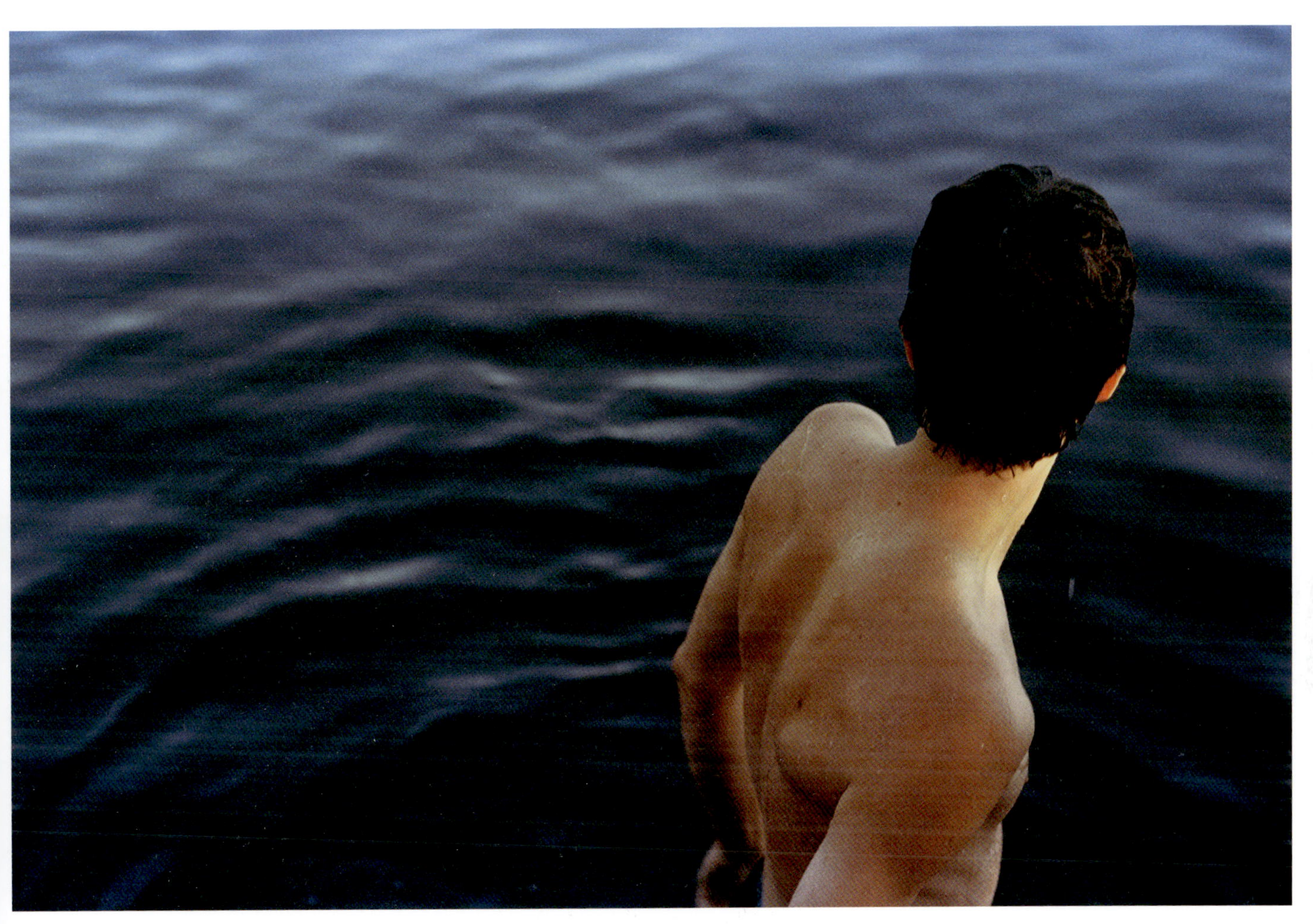

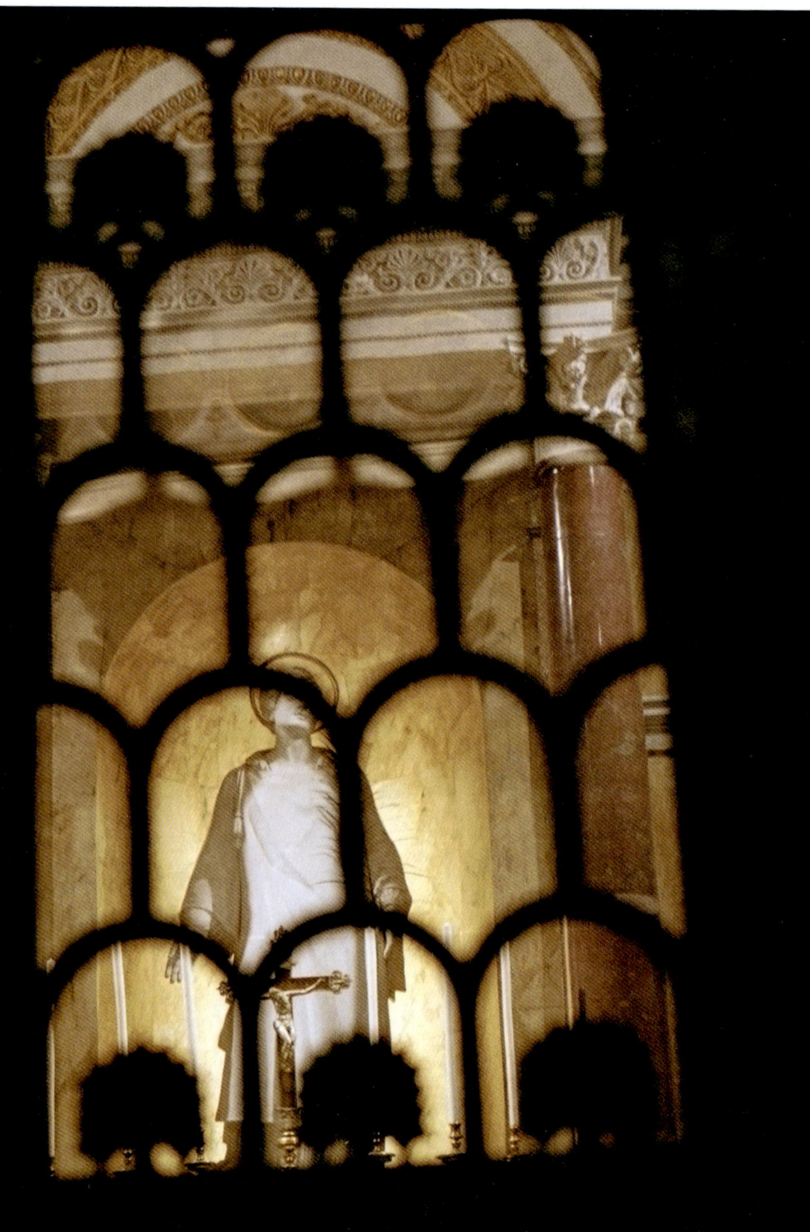

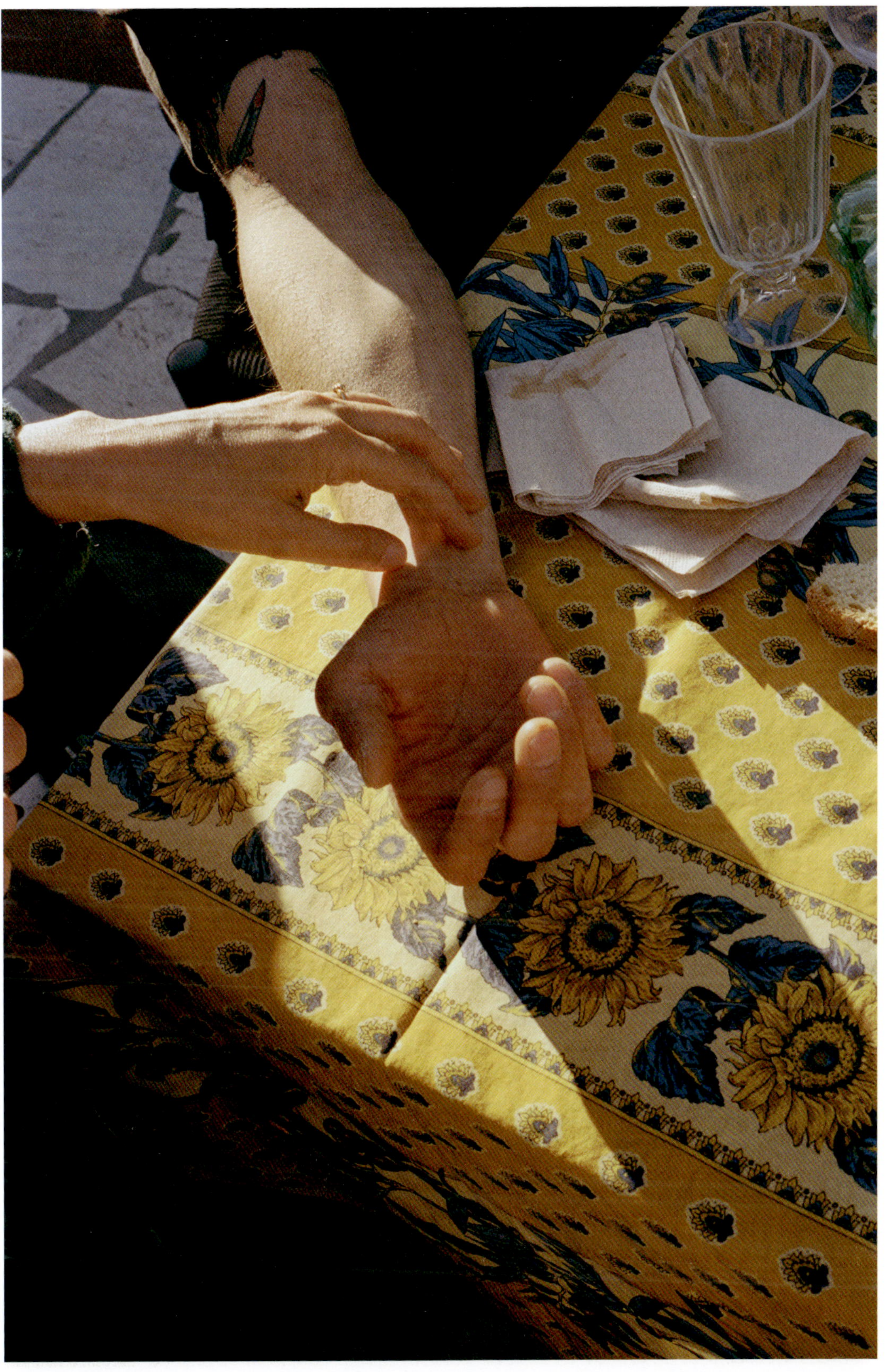

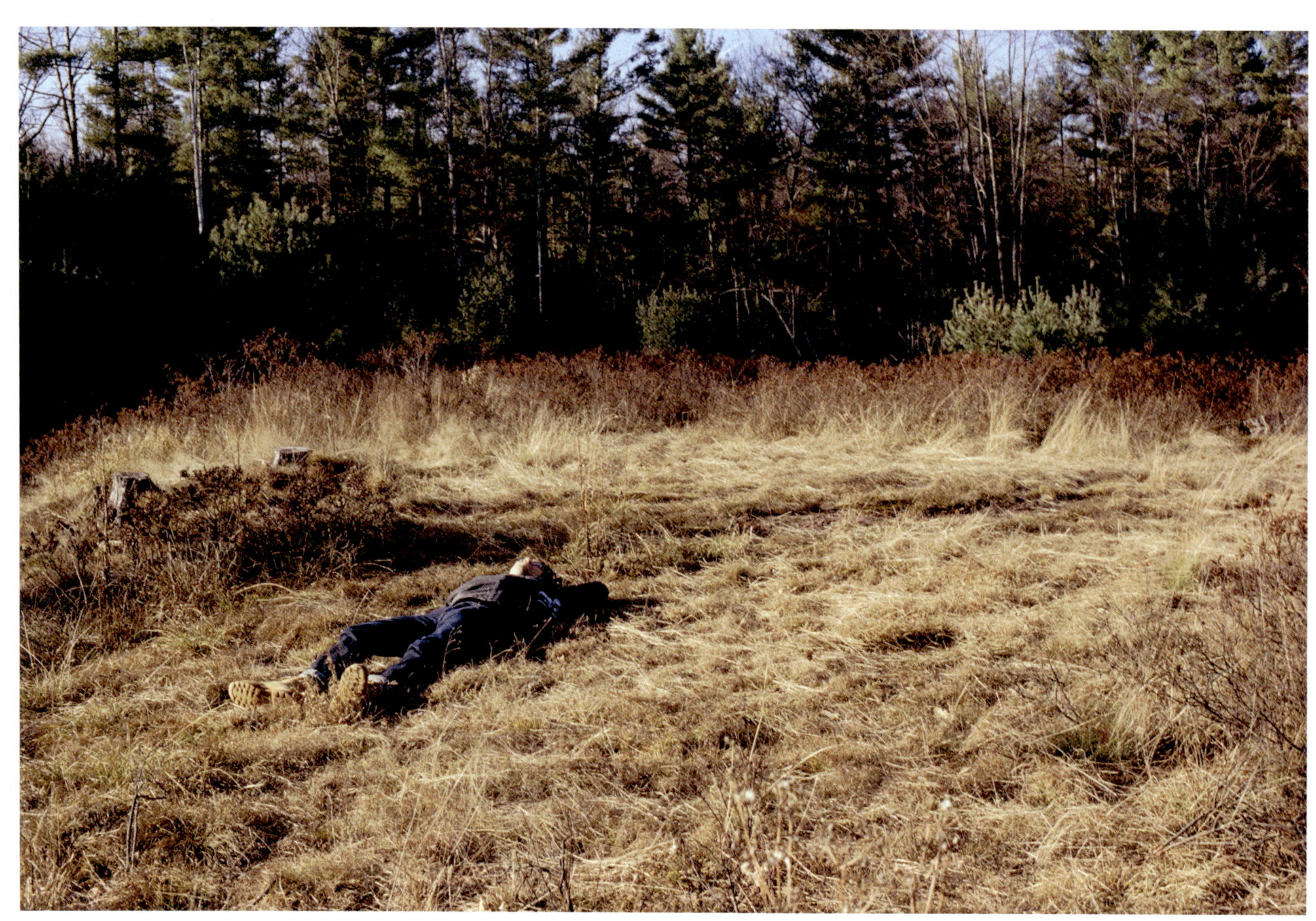

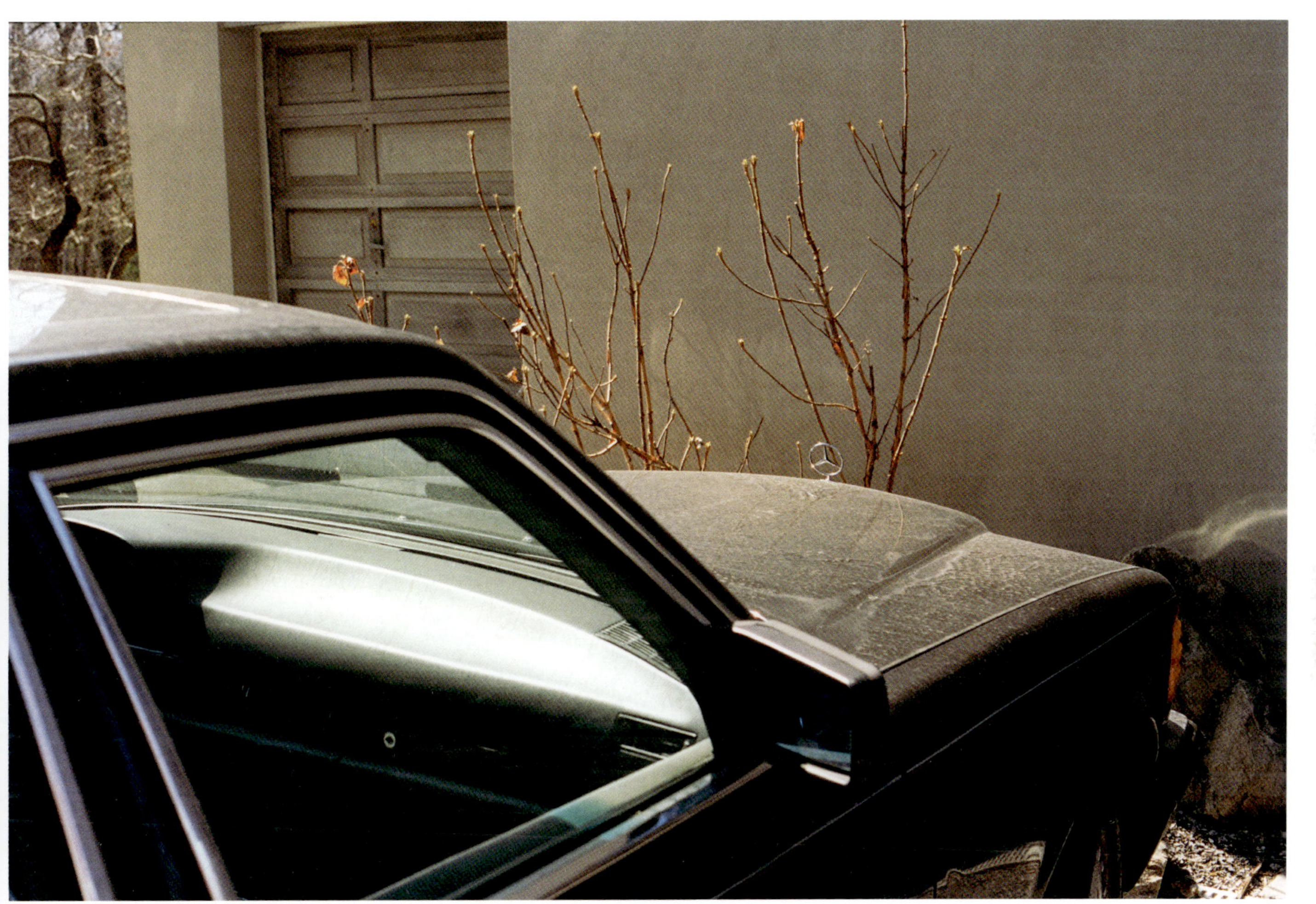

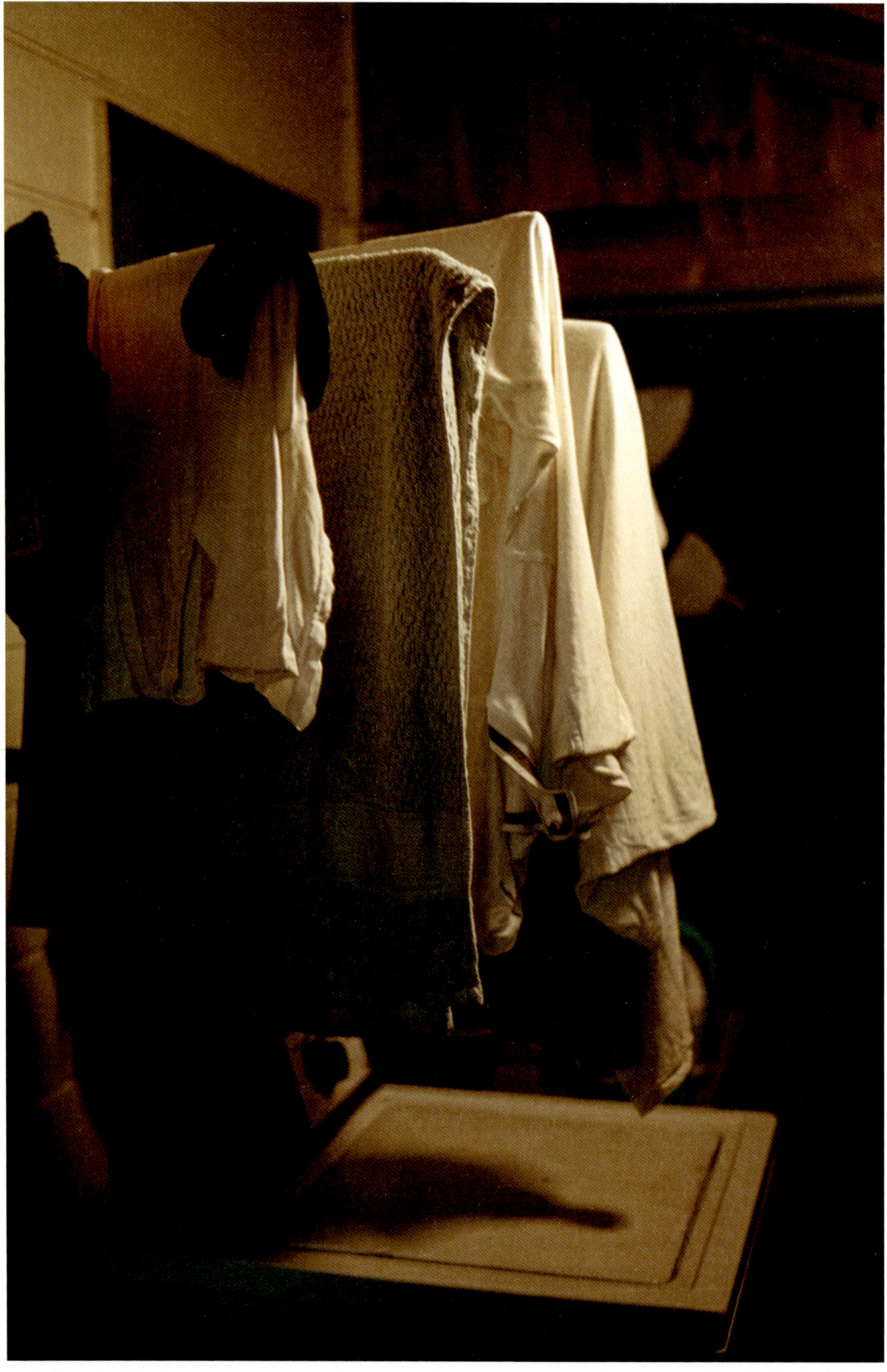

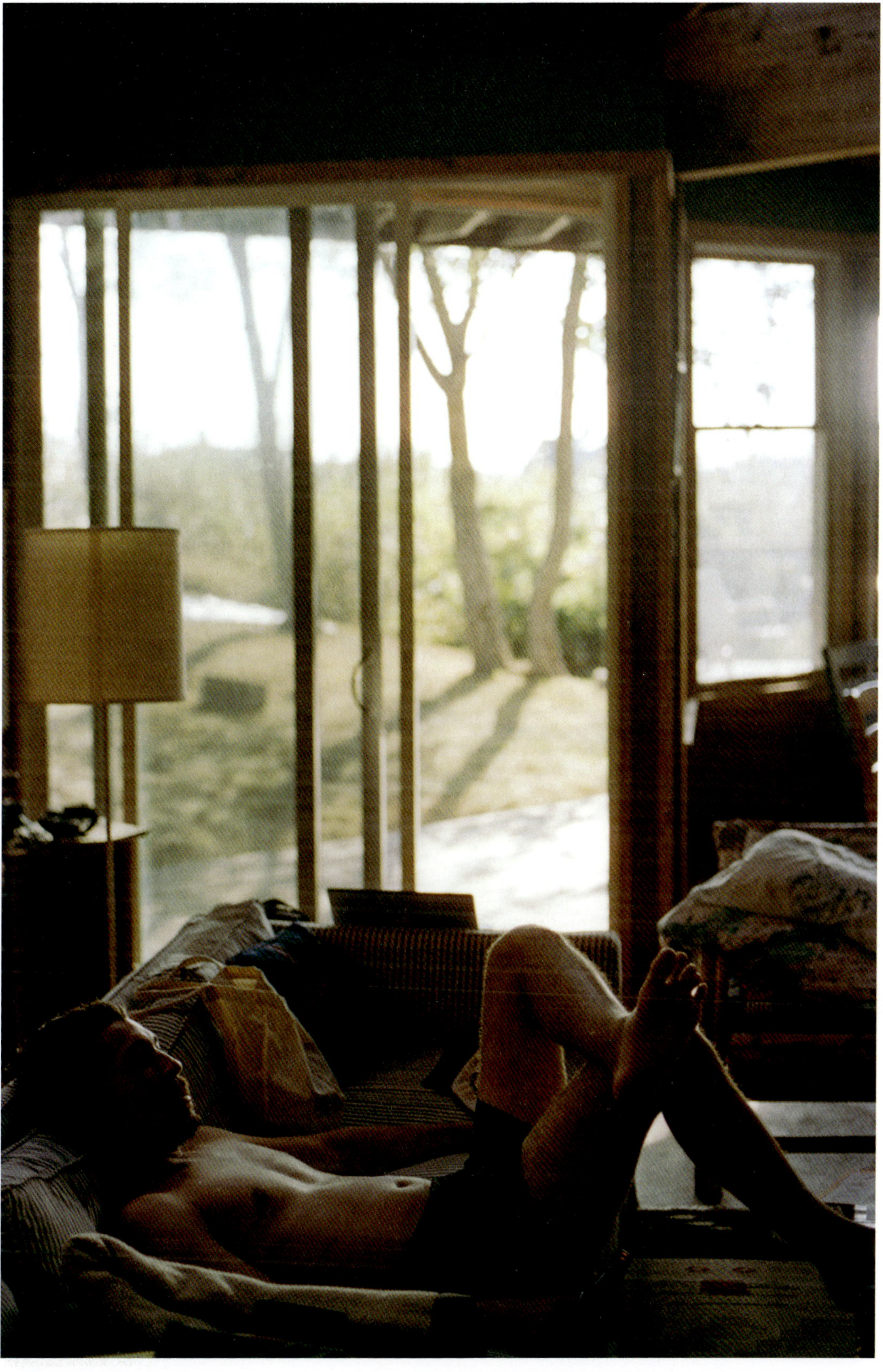

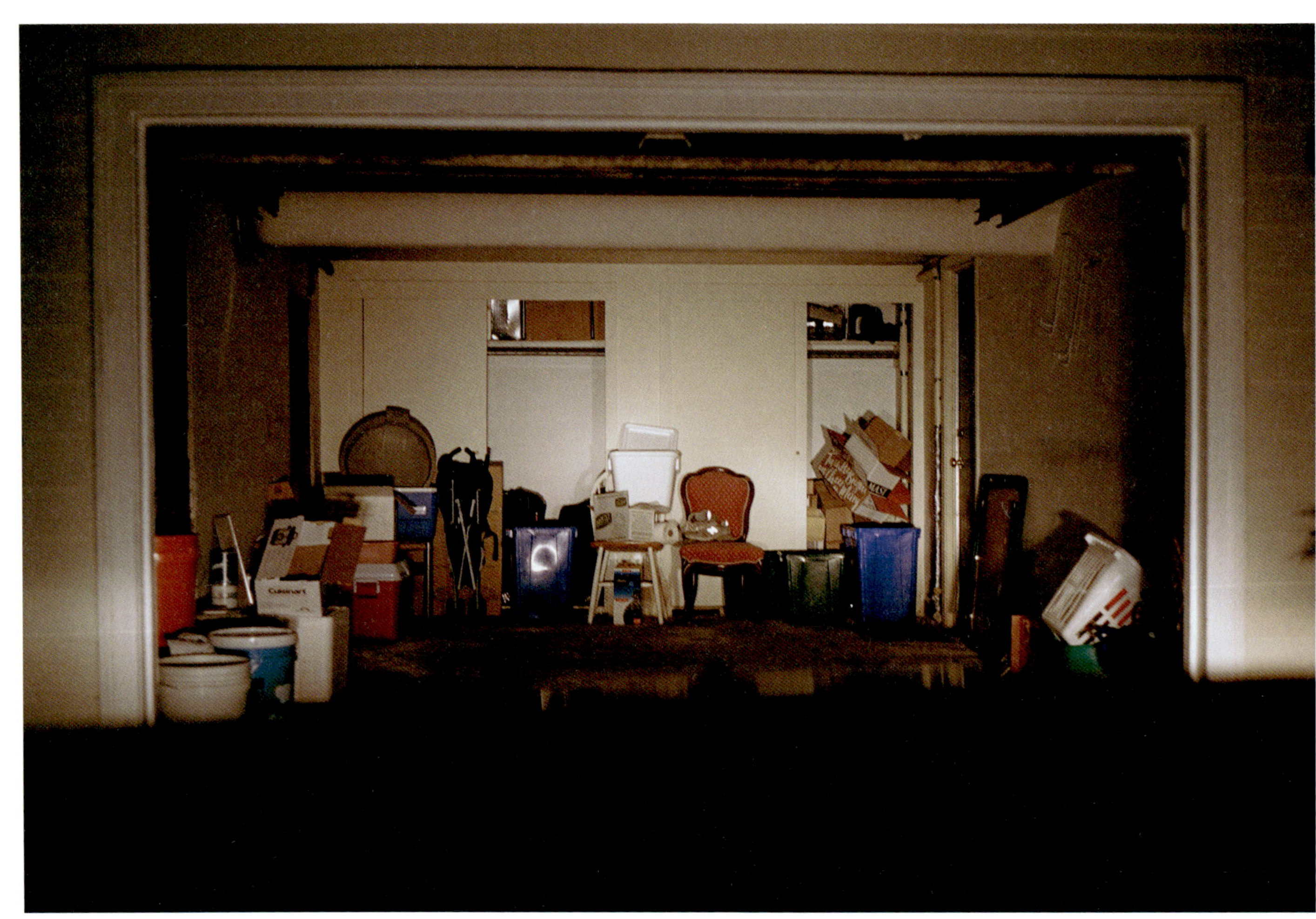

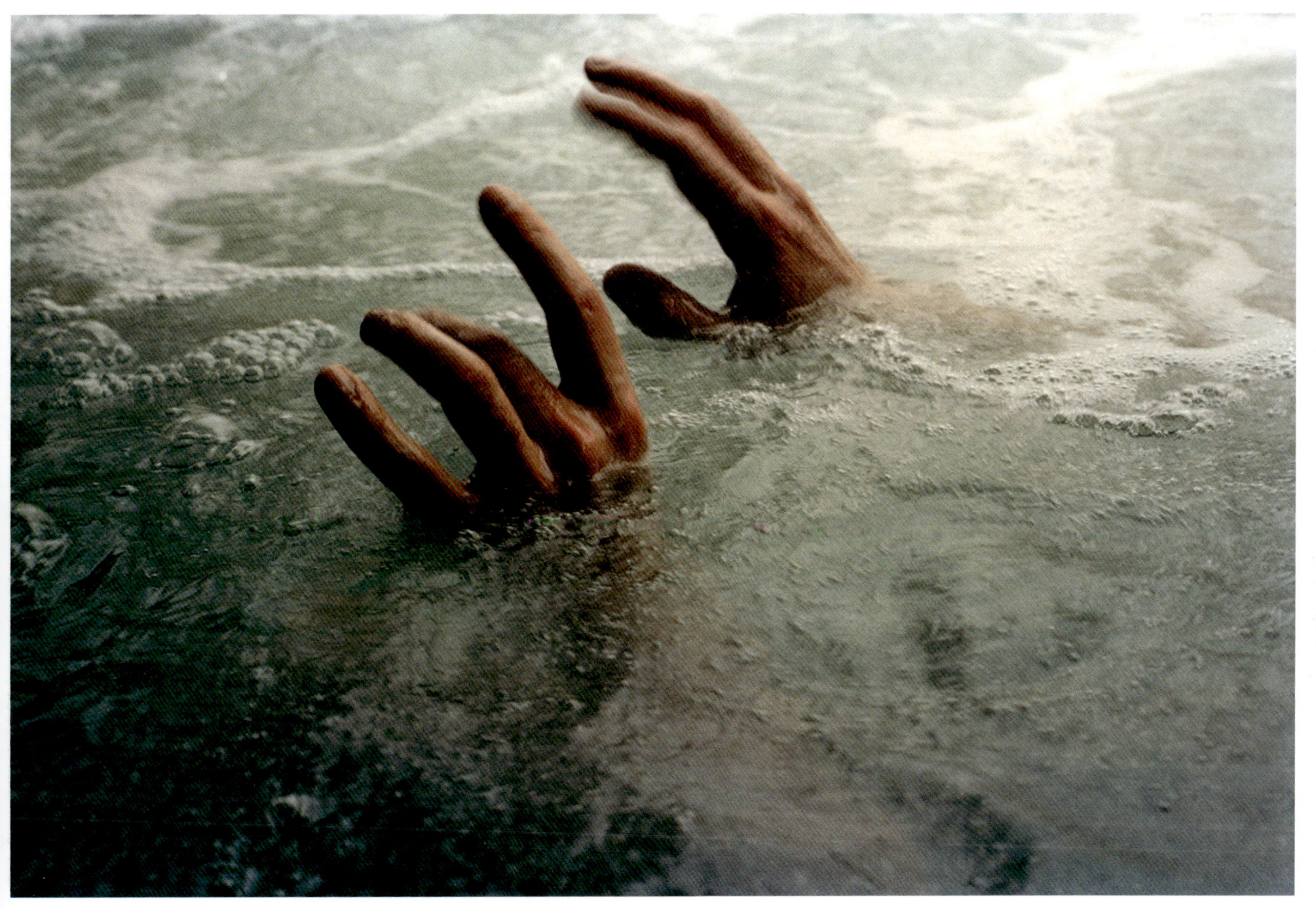

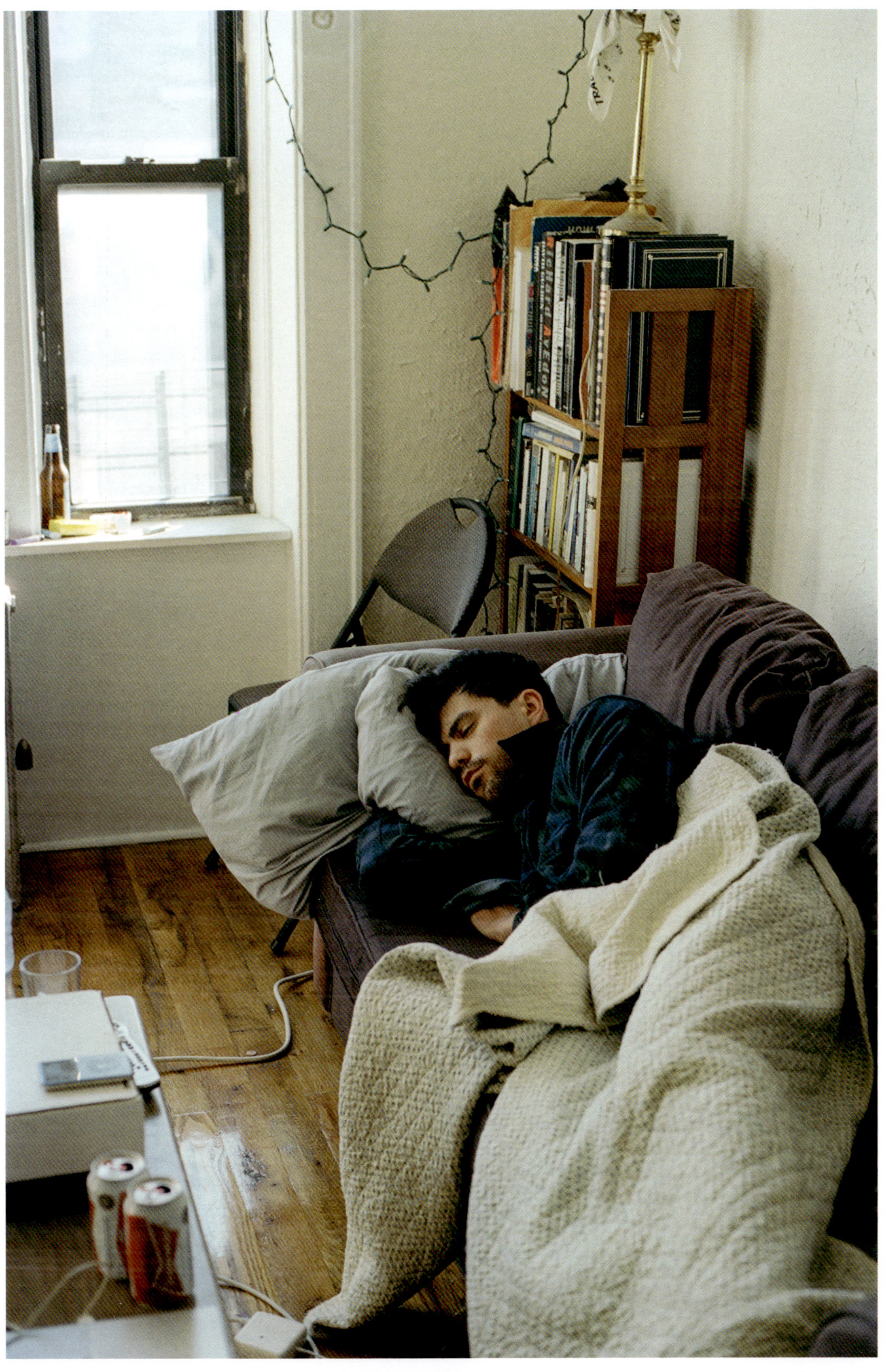

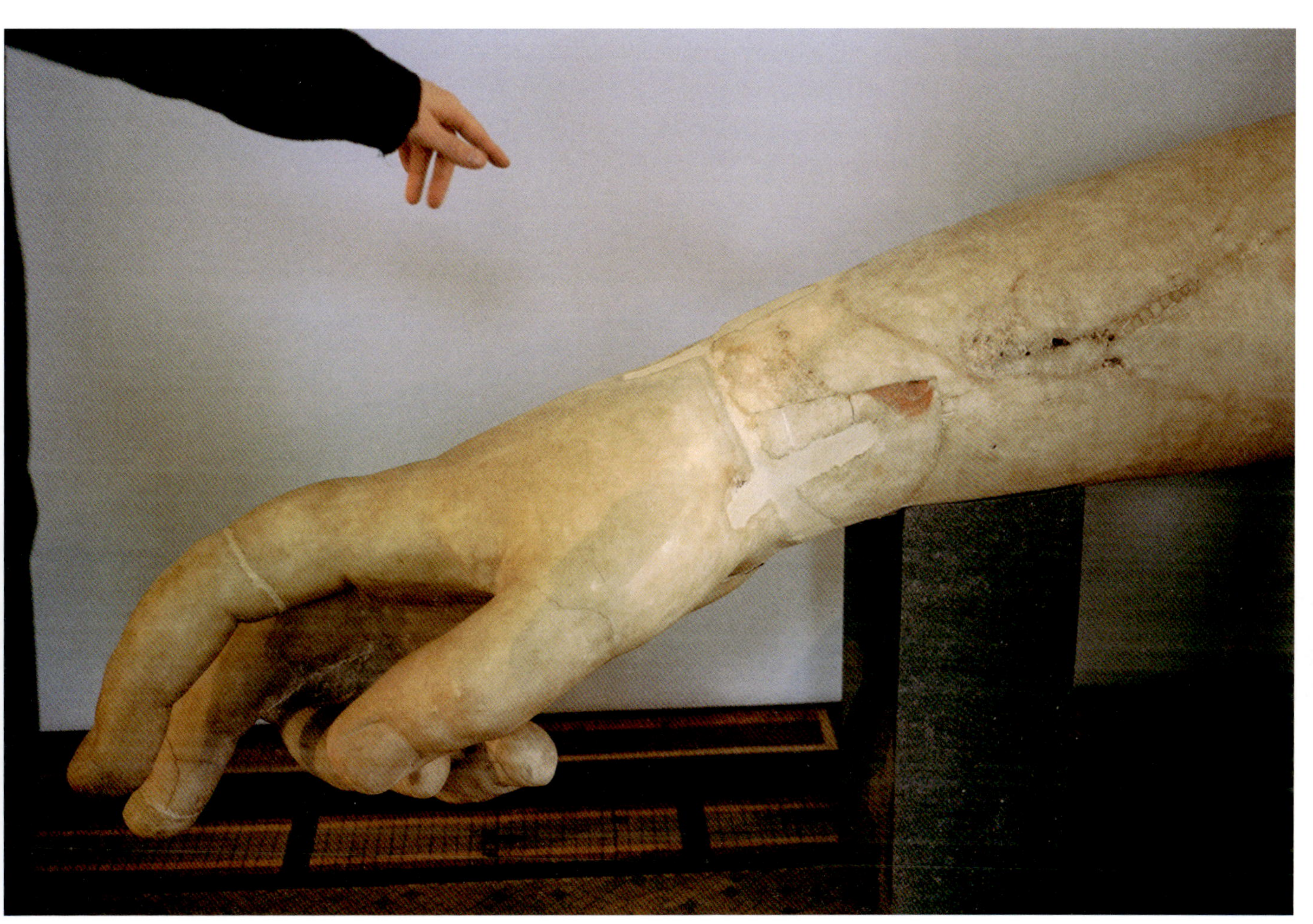

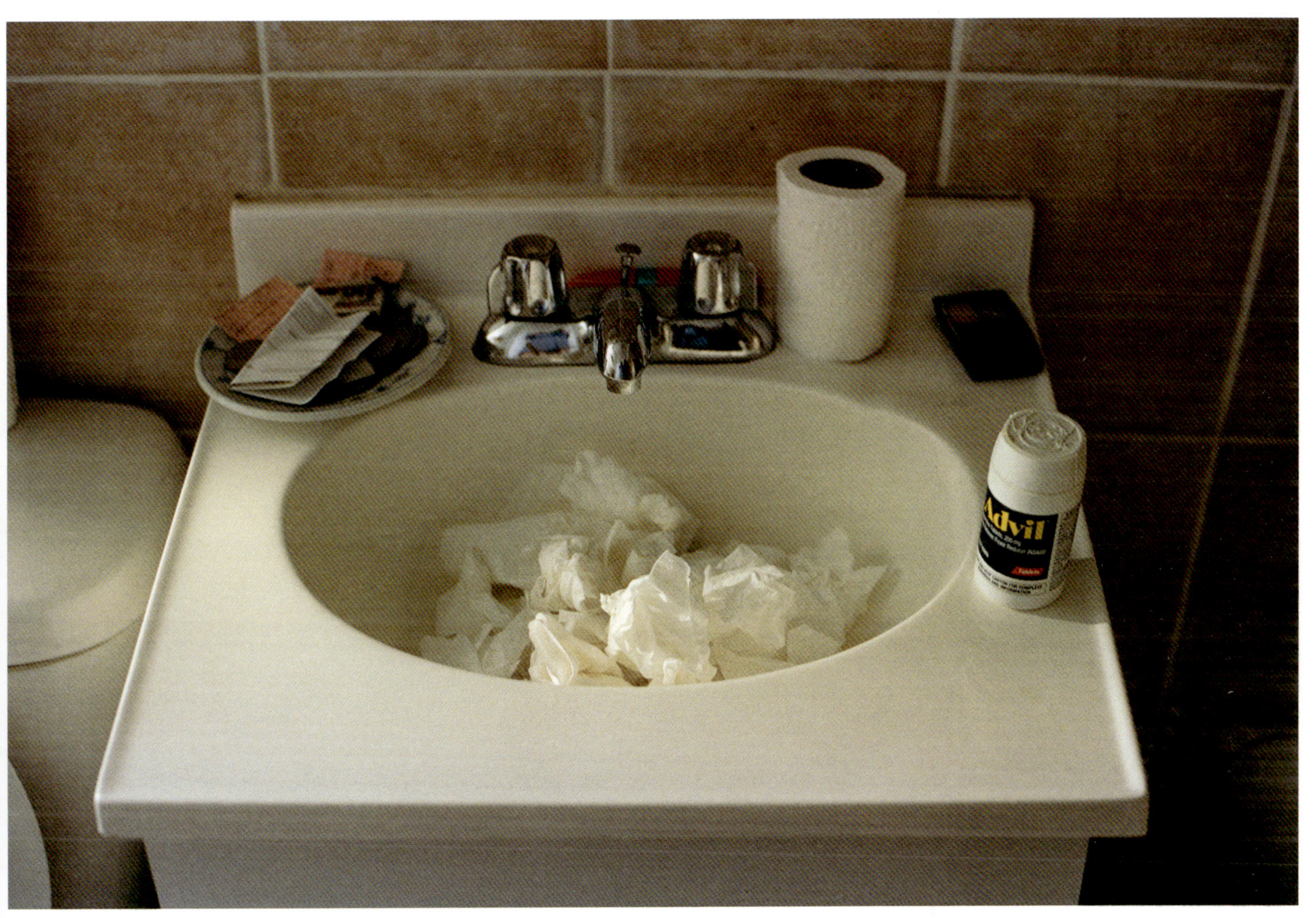

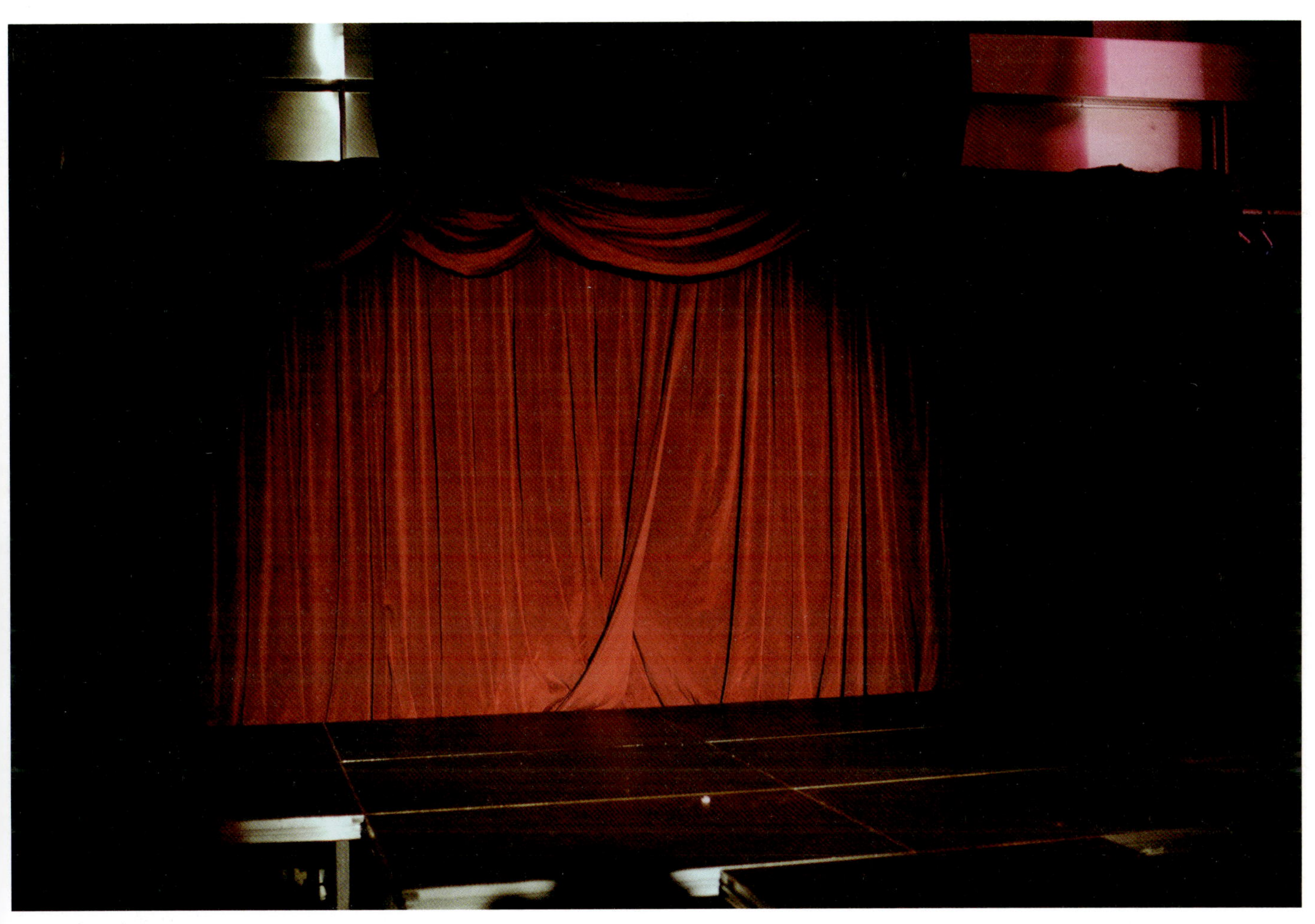

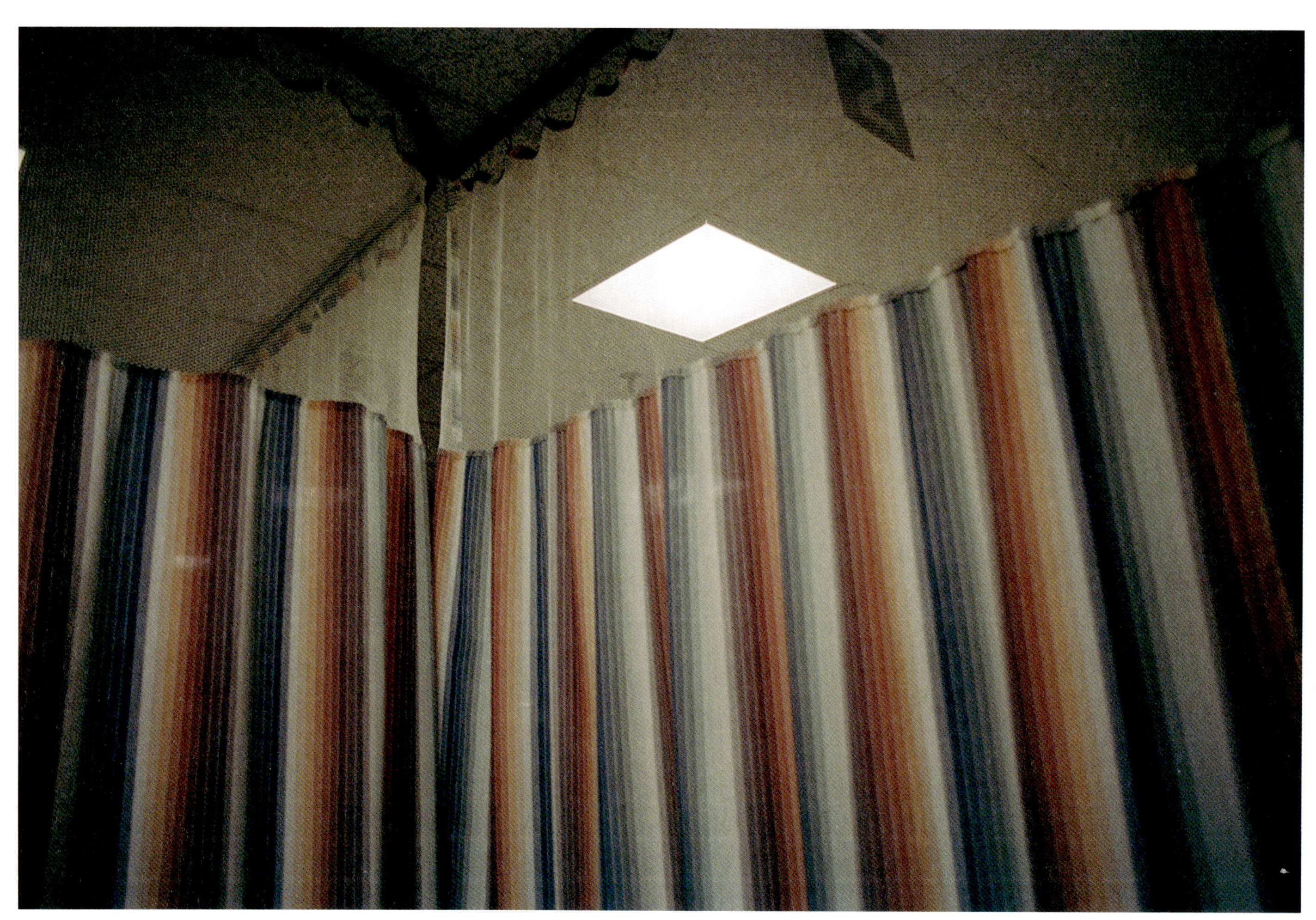

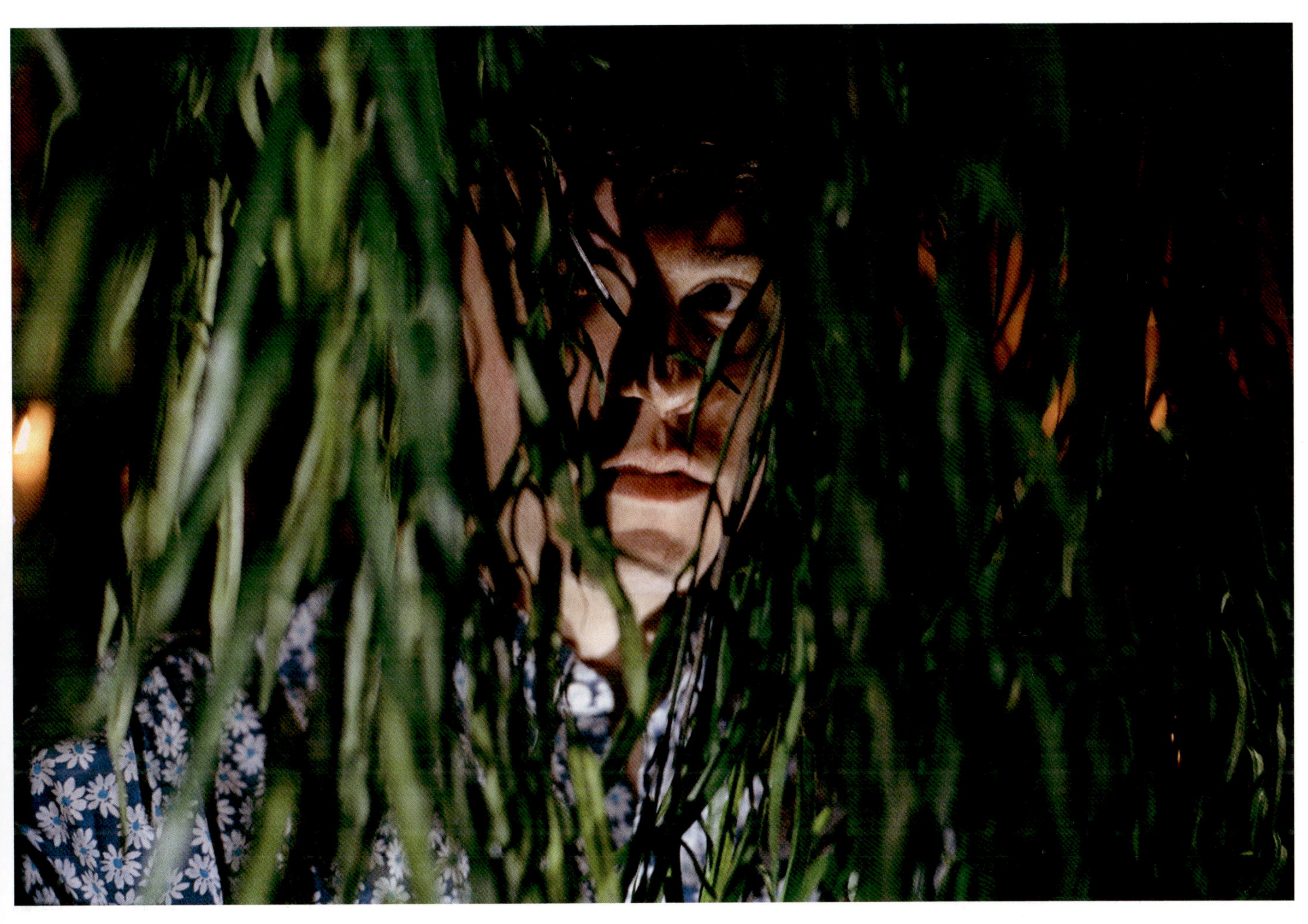

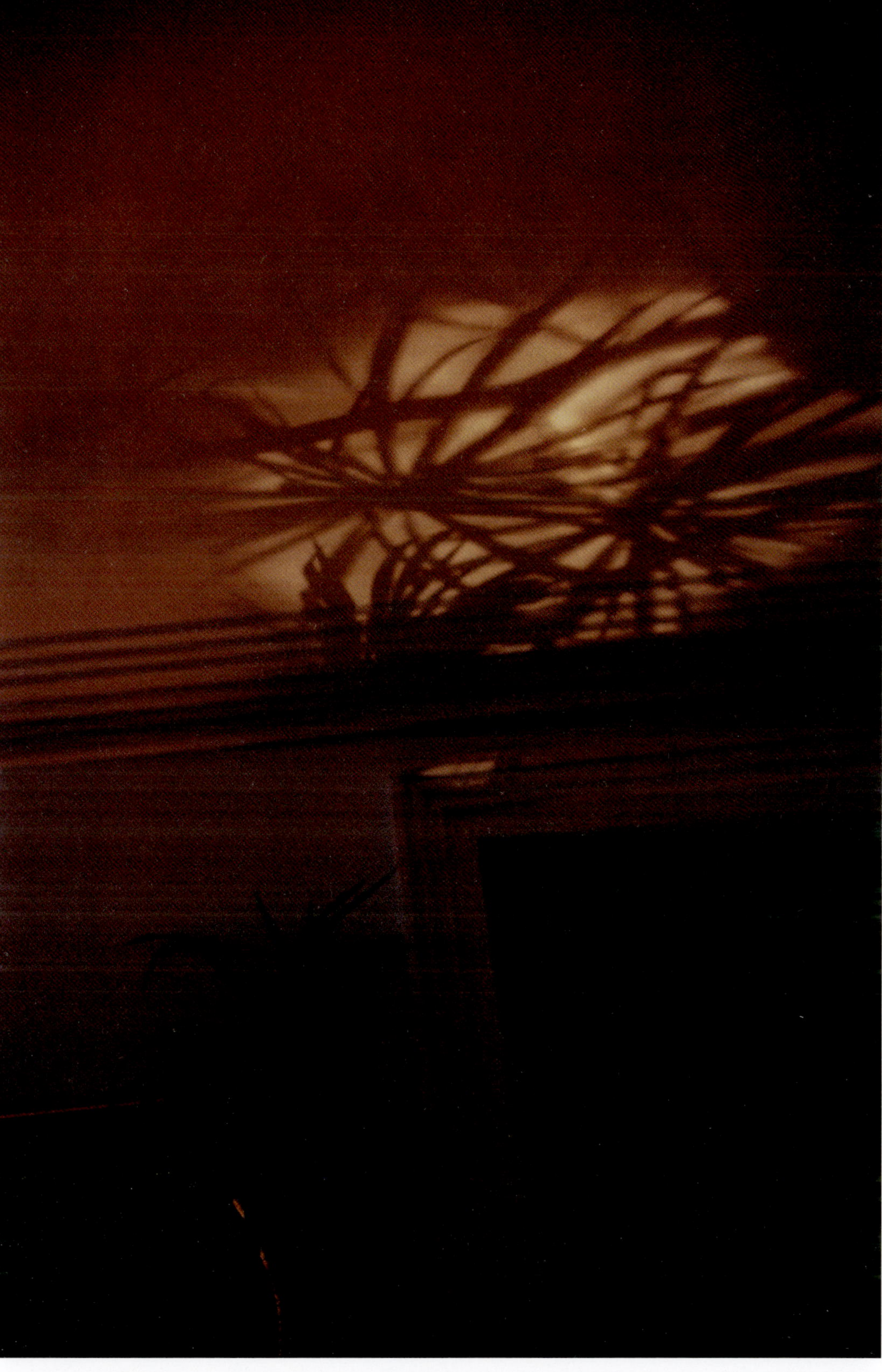

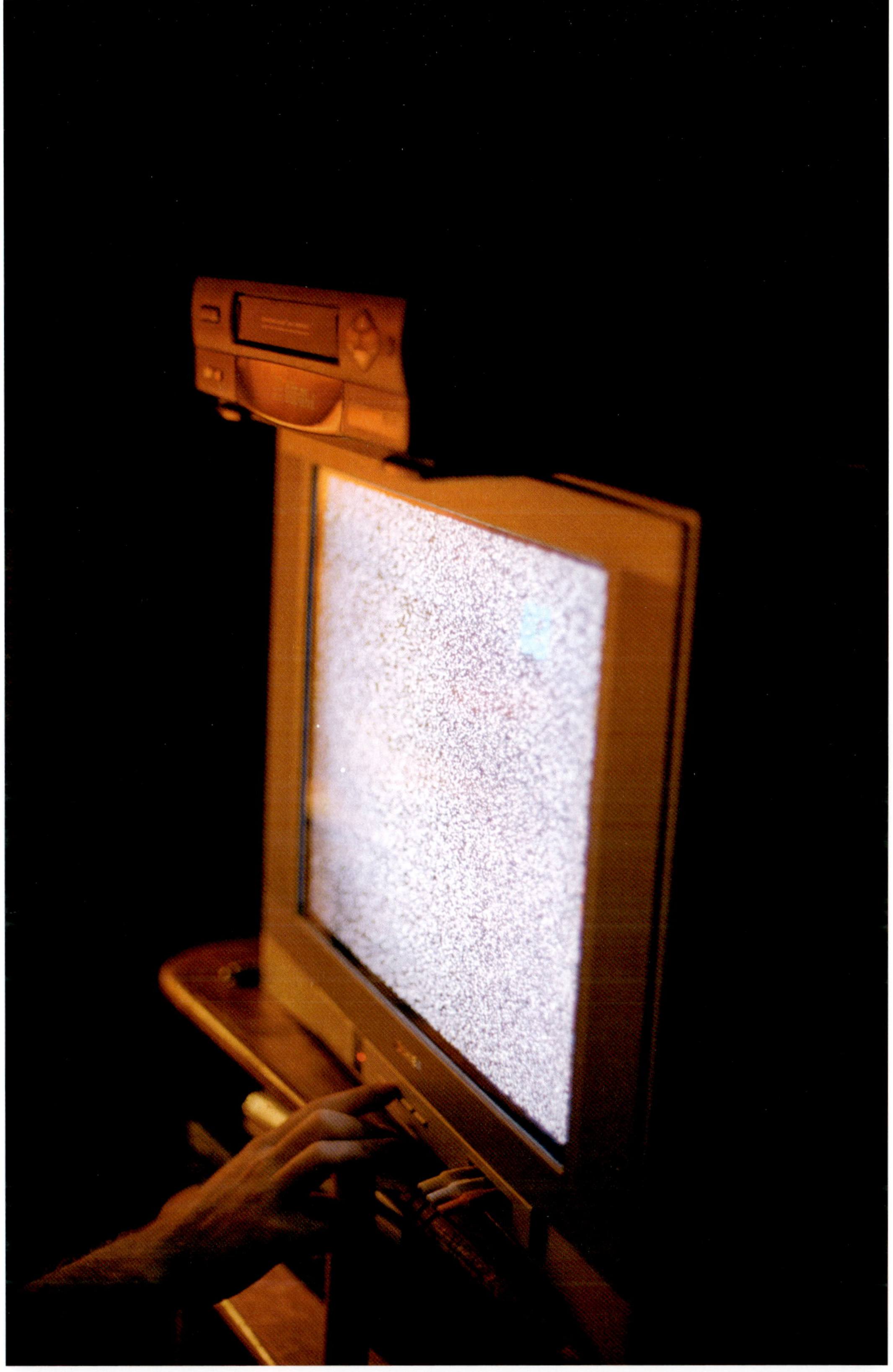

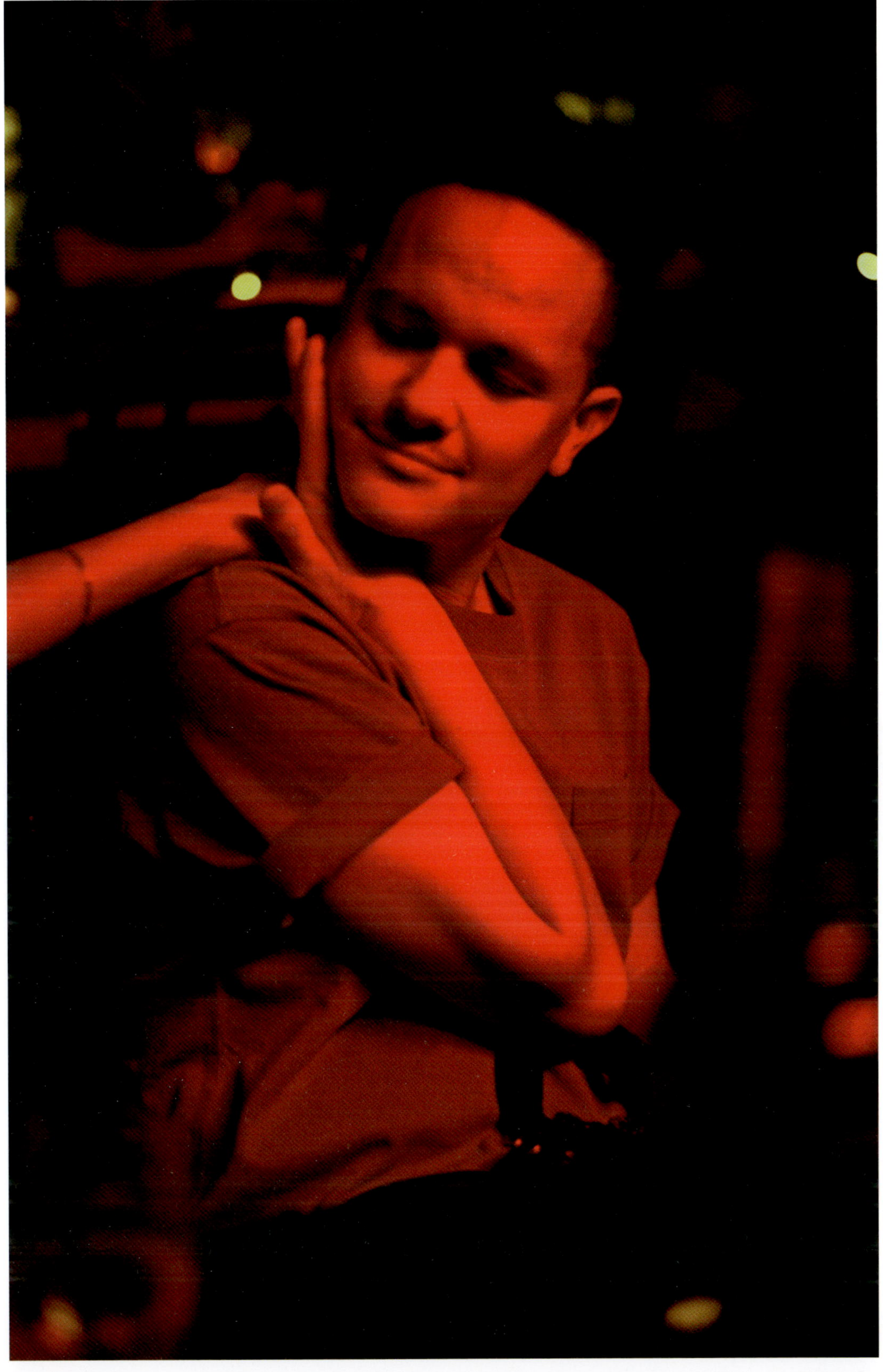

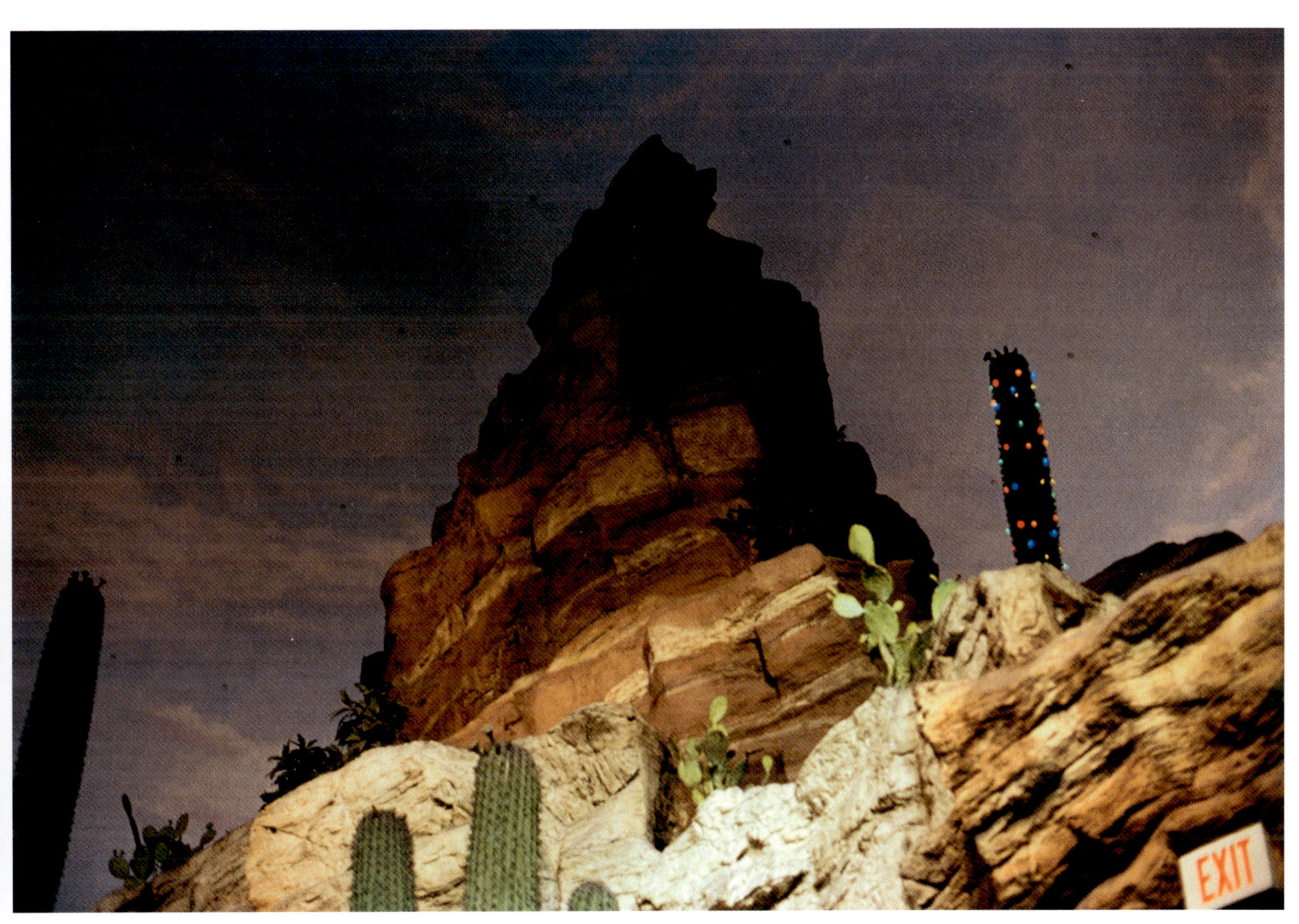
EXIT

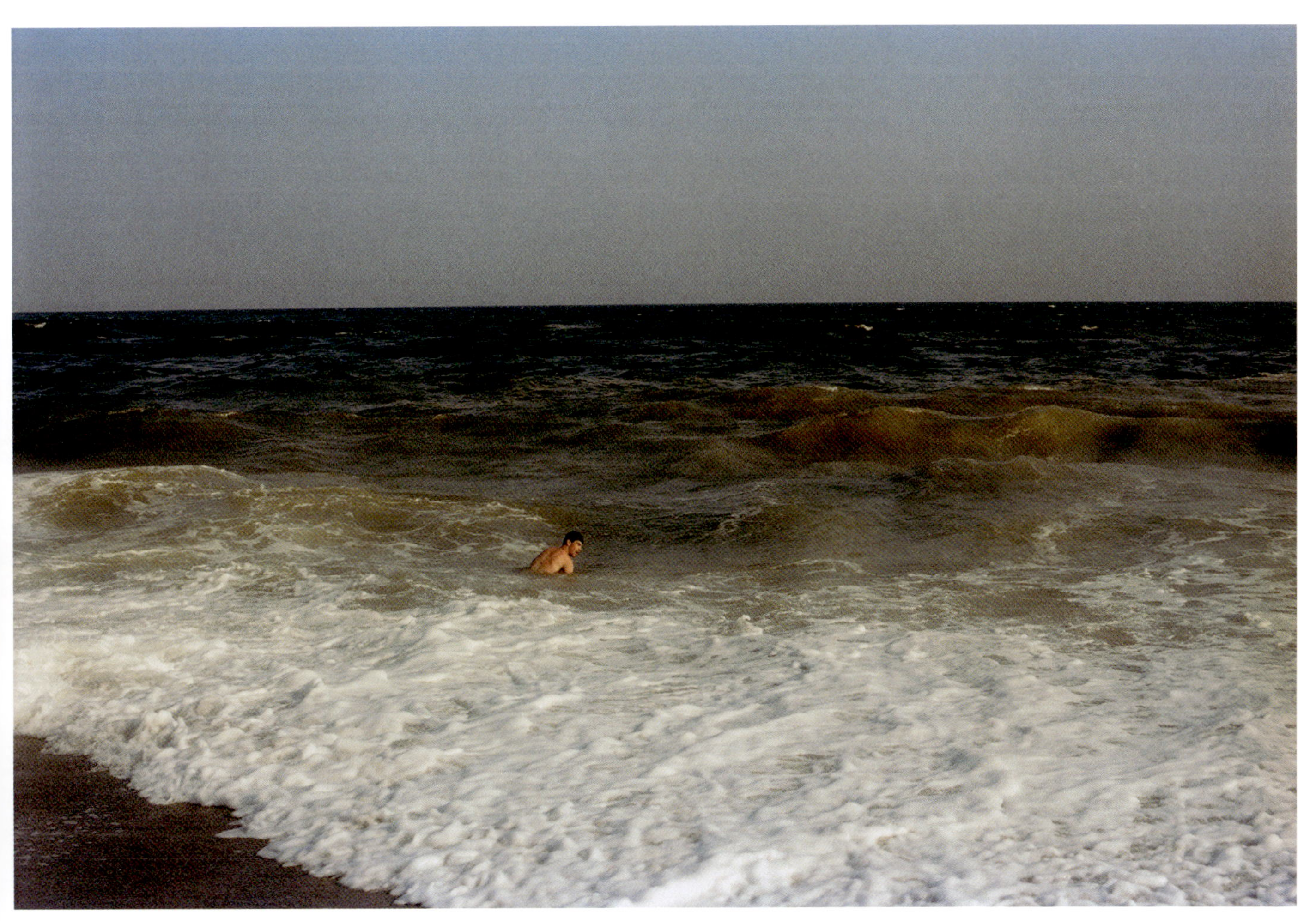

For my family, who takes care of everything:
Clyde & Jacqueline, Paul & Hilary, Judith & George,
Madeleine, Charlotte, Juliette, Eleanor, Abraham,
and Maggie

Yo Cuomo, Sylvia Plachy, Bobbie Richardson,
Silvia Pesci, and for Andrea Albertini
and Matthew Starring

Sonya Belakhlef, Mike Berlin, Victor Blue, Talia Chetrit,
Maria Cobb, Manu Coclin, Peter Curtis,
Charles Damga, Annalisa D'Angelo, Blaine Davis,
Mark Davis, Jessica Foreman, Molly Grassini,
Christian Hansen, Melissa Harris, Dana Michele Hemes,
Malcolm Hill, Monique Jaques, Mike Kamber,
Cory Kamson, Ani Kington, Rachel Klein, Niko Koppel,
Collin LaFleche, Fred LaPolla, Isaac Lavoie, Paolo Lecca,
Joan Liftin, Catherine Litke, Sara Mac, Matt Martin,
Yuta Nakajima, Denis Nazarov, Roman Nazarov,
Anna Parlet, Tomie Peaslee, Paolo Pellegrin,
Igor Posner, Jonno Rattman, Damien Saatdjian,
Caroline Schiff, Anna Serota, Robert Sukrachand,
Eva Tolkin, Nina Toor, Peter van Agtmael,
Mackenzie Wagoner, Jesse Walden, Liv Walton,
Andrew Whyte, and Monica Wu

Bonnie Briant
Lump Sum Lottery

Book design by Bonnie Briant
Cover concept in collaboration with Bobbie Richardson
Editing and sequence by Peter Curtis

Published by Damiani
info@damianieditore.com
www.damianieditore.com

Printed in October 2020, Italy.

ISBN 978-88-6208-723-0

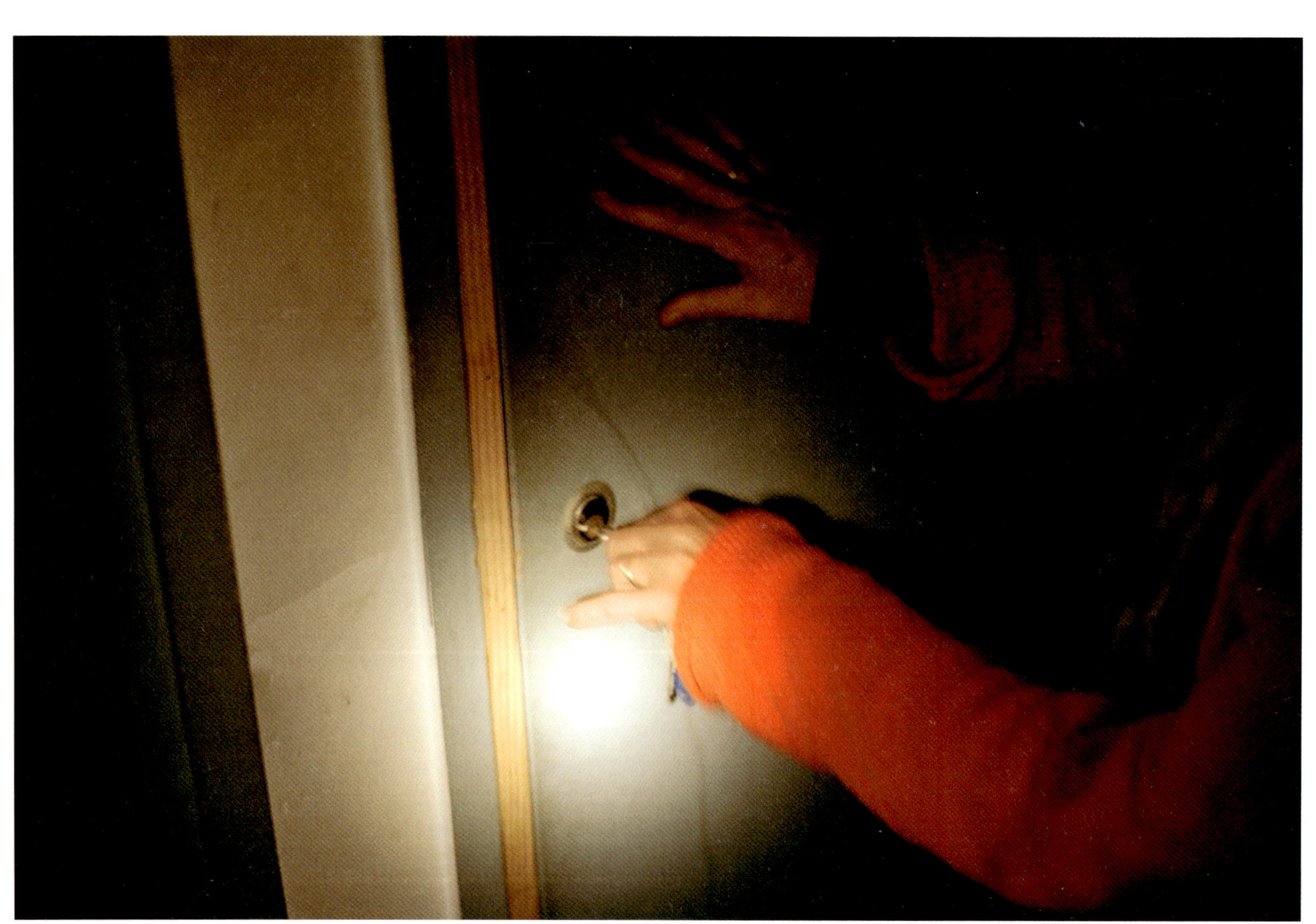